Elizabeth Barton

Inspired TO DESIGN

Seven Steps to Successful Art Quilts

C&T PUBLISHING

Text and Photography copyright © 2013 by Elizabeth Barton

Artwork copyright © 2013 by C&T Publishing, Inc.

PUBLISHER: Amy Marson

CREATIVE DIRECTOR: Gailen Runge

ART DIRECTOR: Kristy Zacharias

EDITOR: Lynn Koolish

TECHNICAL EDITOR: Alison M. Schmidt

COVER/BOOK DESIGNER: April Mostek

PRODUCTION COORDINATOR: Jenny Davis

PRODUCTION EDITOR: Alice Mace Nakanishi

ILLUSTRATOR: Jessica Jenkins

Quilt and Inspirational Photography by Elizabeth Barton, unless otherwise noted; How-To Photography by Christina Carty-Francis and Diane Pedersen of C&T Publishing, Inc.

Published by C&T Publishing, Inc., P.O. Box 1456, Lafayette, CA 94549

Library of Congress Cataloging-in-Publication Data

Barton, Elizabeth, 1949-

Inspired to design : seven steps to successful art quilts / Elizabeth Barton.

  pages cm

ISBN 978-1-60705-634-8 (soft cover)

1. Quilting. 2. Art quilts--Design. I. Title.

TT835.B27555 2013

746.46--dc23

                2012037628

Printed in China

10 9 8 7 6 5 4 3 2 1

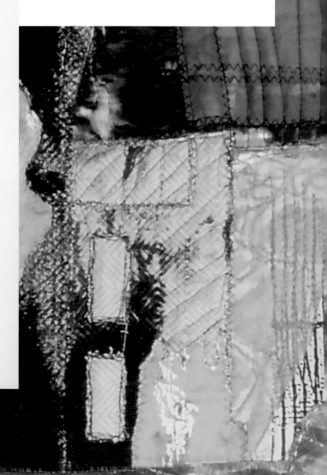

Dedication

For Clare and Jane

Acknowledgments

Thank you to Carol Miller and to Lynn Koolish who encouraged me to write this book. Much gratitude goes to all the students in the workshops I've taught who have been so welcoming and so responsive.

CONTENTS

Introduction

Have you ever wondered how to create an art quilt from a beautiful inspiration such as a gorgeous photograph, a memory of a lovely place, or even an evening drinking and dancing your heart out? The goal of this book is to show you how to work from those inspirations and at the same time help you to discover your own personal voice. It's *your* inspiration and you want *your* voice to express what you saw, heard, smelled, and experienced. It can be so satisfying to make something that shows your own feelings about the flowers in your garden, the day on the river, or the wintry walk.

It's also important to create well-designed and well-composed quilts, so in the process of showing you how to develop designs from your own inspirations, this book will also cover the basics of good design that are relevant to the art quilt.

I often see people writing in their blogs these days, "Oh, don't forget the E's and P's of good design!" I fear they confuse these terms, for they are not the same thing. The E's, or elements, of design are simply the objects that are available to use in two-dimensional design: shapes, lines, values, colors, and textures. Everything in a work of art, be it a quilt, painting, or photograph, is made up of these five basic elements. Every design is made of shapes and lines that are of various colors and values; some of them have a significant pattern (or texture) while others

do not. The elements are the building blocks. They are *what* you work with, so they're not something you're likely to forget! In quilts, shapes are made from fabric, but they are still just shapes; stitches are lines. Textures can be the design printed or painted onto the surface of the fabric, or the density of the quilting.

The P's, or principles, refer to *how well* you arrange the elements in two-dimensional space. The principles, simply listed, are unity/harmony, variety, rhythm/repetition/movement, balance/proportion, and economy. There is much more to come about the importance of these concepts.

We'll go through all the steps from the initial idea or inspiration through the formulation of a strong composition. It's a step-by-step approach because a great composition does not happen by accident. It takes planning, patience, and knowledge. It requires you to think. Every step in creating a quilt design involves choices, and choices are determined by the power of thought.

After you've had a lot of experience with looking and designing, however, many of the steps and things you have to watch out for become more automatic. This is why experienced artists often appear to be working quickly and effortlessly—what you don't see is the hours and hours, weeks, months, and years of practice. Making art is the same as playing the piano or dancing ballet: It requires practice.

West Cliff Steps, the original photo, by Elizabeth Barton

West Cliff Steps by Elizabeth Barton, 40″ × 63″

Step 1:
Inspirations and Design Sketches

GETTING STARTED

The goal of this first section of the book is to help you develop at least a dozen designs. Don't worry! You won't be making them all! Once you have the designs, you will learn how to evaluate them, but at first, all you need to do is generate as many ideas as you can. It's helpful to pin them up so that you can look them over every time you go into your studio or sewing area. You can sneak in for a quick peek several times a day. So put them up as soon as you come up with the ideas. Try to be loose and experimental. You've only a piece of paper to lose. No expensive material is wasted. The exercises in this section will help you generate design sketches, so use them to your advantage.

And, *no criticizing!* Instead, think about covering the wall with designs. They need to be clear enough so that you can stand back a little to look at them, so if you work in pencil, you might want to go over the pencil lines with a marker to make them more visible. It's helpful to keep them to a standard size—a letter-size piece of paper (8½″ × 11″) is good. If you come up with a design that is significantly smaller, enlarge it using a photocopier so it matches the others.

The only essential initial supplies are an inspiration notebook, a pencil, and paper. While a light table, a photocopier, and a photo-editing program such as Photoshop are helpful and I use them quite a lot, they are definitely *not* necessary, so don't worry if you don't have them. My approach involves using time and thought, not spending a lot of money.

Design Wall

A design wall is simply a vertical space where you can compose quilts. Why vertical? Because you are making an art quilt that will be hung, and therefore seen, vertically when it is finished. Thus, it is important that when you make decisions about all aspects of the design, you are looking from the same perspective as the final piece.

My design walls are simply 4′ × 8′ sections of insulation foam that are tacked onto the wall. They are covered with batting, although Polartec fleece or flannel would work just as well. If space is restricted, you do not need to fasten the foam board to the wall. Instead, store it and take it out

Sketches pinned up for consideration on design wall

when you need to work on it. I like a big space, so I have three sections of foam board, but really all you need is one piece a little bigger all around than the quilt you wish to make.

Inspiration Notebook

The most important piece of equipment is the inspiration notebook. And these are so much fun to make. I've often had people bring three or four to a class!

It is rare for an artist to compose in a void; everyone needs a starting point. Picasso, Monet, Renoir, and Vermeer did not go off to work, pull out a blank canvas, and compose something wonderful out of their heads, so you shouldn't expect to either.

If you haven't already, start collecting inspirations such as photographs, paintings, color combinations—anything that intrigues you. You've probably already got many of these lying around. Put each inspiration into a sheet protector in a binder or glue it onto a page in a scrapbook. I like the sheet protectors because you can then easily pull out an item to photocopy it in black and white, enlarge it, or trace it—it's just easier to handle than if it's glued. Also, you can pull out a dozen or so as you look through your books and pin them up to look at as a whole. Include notes on specific experiences or doodles you make while

One of many pages in my inspiration notebook

on the telephone. If it catches your eye, put it in your inspiration notebook. I've sometimes torn out an idea for a color sequence or just the pattern of a T-shirt from a clothing advertisement. When something piques your interest, it is grist to the mill, manure for the garden.

It's a good idea to include pictures of quilts you have made that you feel were your most successful and from which you can learn and develop other ideas. I think it is also helpful to include a few pictures of other people's quilts that you really admire, but try to include a variety of quilts by different people so that you do not get influenced too much by one particular quilter. You want to develop your own voice, not imitate another's style. Don't have too many pictures of quilts, either—it's much harder to develop original ideas from your own real-time experiences if you're already viewing "predigested" ones!

Just to get you started, here is a page from my own inspiration notebook as an inspiration.

Idea of a City by Elizabeth Barton, 60″ × 60″   *From the Top* by Elizabeth Barton, 45″ × 46″

MAKING NOTES

As you enjoy a cup of tea or a glass of wine, with your feet up, look at your inspirational pictures one by one and write down what it is about this photo, sketch, or painting that really impresses and fascinates you. For example, with a photo of a city it might be the interesting interlocking of the buildings.

If it is a landscape, it might be the dynamic planes, peacefulness, or special sense of place that caught your eye.

In a still life, the repetition of a particular shape or pattern may be the most intriguing thing—or perhaps the way the different elements interact with each other. In a field of poppies it could be the bright red against the green, or it could be the jaunty way the flowers hold their heads up, or the sense of the breeze causing them to dance. There are so many possibilities. Each one is personal, but it is also often fleeting, and that's why it's important to *note it down*. It is difficult to have a good composition without having *something to compose about*, and the notes help you to see what was important to you.

If you are going out with a camera to capture inspirational photos for your notebook, try to think about the light as you take the pictures. A good range of lights and darks will really help to support your composition. An artist friend of mine takes all her photos in seasons and at times of day when the sun is at a low angle in the sky—this way she makes sure that her inspirational photos have a lot of luscious darks and lights.

The Main Idea or Theme

The first step in creating any art is to figure out what the main idea is. What do you want to make a quilt about? What has caught your eye or your heart? It can be something small, like a bowl of cherries or a few leaves dancing in the wind with the light shining through; it could be the feelings of joy at the birth of a child or horror at war; or it could be a fascination with mathematical puzzles or with the way words look on a page. It can be depicted in a realistic, representational, or quite abstract manner. Don't feel that you have to decide how you're going to show the main idea right away. Trying to think about how you'll take the fifth step when you're only taking the second one can lead to stumbling.

It is important to know what your overall idea is when you set out to make art. Otherwise it could be like the proverbial monkeys trying to type a Shakespeare play: Eventually, by randomly hitting keys, they might do it—well, perhaps a quotation or two—but there is so much room for error, so many possibilities, that more likely they will end up with nonsense. When we were kids, my brother and I went for long walks. Usually we would say, "Today we will walk to the hilly fields" or "Today we will go to the pond by the river." We reached those places and enjoyed those walks. We went to the hilly fields when we wanted to roll down them, and that was the feeling of the day. The pond by the river was for quieter times, when we would lie on our stomachs, hanging out over the water and watching the tadpoles and minnows. But sometimes we felt lazy and we'd say, "Let the dog decide." And of course the dog went the same way every time—straight to the butcher shop. Or occasionally in a circle around her favorite sniffing spots! On the days that we let the dog choose, we went nowhere!

So think before you set out: What are you trying to convey? What is the experience that you want? Almost every other decision you will make about the piece will be informed by the main idea. Remember—it can be realistic

Pump Court by Elizabeth Barton, 35" × 48"

or completely abstract. Beatle George Harrison opened one of his mother's romantic novels and began a song from the phrase "gently weeps" that caught his eye. I made the quilt *Pump Court* (above) because I was thinking about the little alleyways in my hometown and how much they revealed the age and the medieval character of the city. I cast a blue light over the piece by overdyeing it, which I hoped would make it a little more distant and mysterious.

In her book *The Creative Habit*, choreographer Twyla Tharp wrote, "Every work of art needs an underlying theme, a motive for coming into existence." Think about it: What *are* you trying to say? What is your intention? It is so helpful to clarify your goals for the piece at the beginning. Tharp's term for the main idea is the *spine* of the piece. (I highly recommend her book, by the way.)

Questions to Ask Yourself about the Inspiration

After you have collected photographs and pictures and notes on music, poetry, or walks in the woods, analyze what it is about this source material that attracts you. Let's assume, for right now, that it is a visual inspiration (though it doesn't have to be—all senses can inspire us to create art). Looking at the inspirational photograph, ask yourself the following questions. Remember that what intrigued you could be more than just one thing. It doesn't have to be world-shattering. Adjust the questions accordingly if your inspiration is an experience, like riding a white horse along the beach or listening to a piece of music.

Sit quietly in front of the inspirational image, think, and ask yourself these questions:

- What in this image seized my eye? The shapes? The colors? The lines? The contrast of light and dark? The texture?

- What is the main idea I want to make a piece about?

- Which parts of the inspiration are most relevant to the main idea and therefore important to include?

- And more importantly, which can, and therefore should, be left out?

Michelangelo supposedly said that he took a block of marble and chipped away what he did *not* want, revealing his sublime inspiration. Now I'm not suggesting that we can all be Michelangelos; however, it's often what is *not* included that is the most important. Making a piece of visual art is a bit like writing a poem—every element should be crucial to the finished piece, and nothing extraneous should be included.

Going back again to your inspiration, here are a few more questions:

- Will other elements need to be added?

- How and where can more pizzazz / oomph / excitement be added in order to make the final work sing?

It isn't necessary to find the answer to this final question before you start, but keep it in mind. And as you look at other examples of artistic endeavor, whether it's quilts, painting, poetry, cooking, gardening, or antique cars, try to identify what it is that makes one stand out against all the others. Sometimes it's the quality of the chiaroscuro (the play of light and dark); another time it's just a few little touches of highly saturated color in a few key places. If you look at Dorothy Caldwell's amazing quilts, you'll see it's often the apparently careless, beautifully carefree, or agonizingly nostalgic quality of a line of stitching.

Not a Copy

Your designs should *not* be a direct copy of the inspiration—a photograph would certainly be a more precise copy. Instead, your designs should be a *translation*. Don't think about literally transcribing color, value, or texture. Think about how composers have translated themes in music in works such as *Flight of the Bumblebee, The Lark Ascending*, or the *1812 Overture*. They did not literally go out and record bumblebees, larks, or cannons! The quilt is your own vision; you can make the sky any color you want. But choose the color wisely. Choose it by thinking about how the color can reflect your main idea, and assess how that sky color will interrelate with all the other colors. The same is true of all the other elements in a quilt. We'll discuss these issues with much more depth in later steps, but I want you to remember that in a work of art, *you are not reporting facts; rather, you are expressing the truth about something as you see and feel it.*

Petra by Elizabeth Barton, 45" × 55"

Petra is an example of a quilt in which it was the color of the stone that really spoke to me. I'd often heard Petra described as "the rose-red city half as old as time" (John William Burgon, 1845) and I wanted to put that idea into the quilt.

Mindfulness

Think about designing with all your senses. Be curious about your subject as a child might be, or a visitor from Mars. Involve yourself slowly and mindfully with the subject. Teachers of mindfulness ask you to put a raisin into your mouth, close your eyes, and think about that raisin from the point of view of *every* sense. How did it look? What does it feel like when your tongue touches it, and how does that feeling change? What is the first taste, and how does the taste develop? Can you smell it? What are your physical sensations as you slowly soften and then eat the raisin? It is having this kind of awareness about your main idea that will help you make a unique piece.

Thinking in Abstract Terms

When you are looking at the inspirational material, use words like *shape, line, value, color*, and *texture* (the elements of design) to help you think in abstract terms. For example, instead of thinking about boats in a harbor as the subject, think of a scattered pattern of red on blue, the harmony of the colors, the sense of space conveyed, the wetness or flatness.

If a house is the main subject, don't think "house"; think squares and rectangles, line, patterns of light and shade, the harmony of the colors, the sense of space conveyed, texture, height and depth. Identify the positive and negative shapes, lines, colors, values, and textures that interest you. If you're looking at children at play on a climbing frame, think about the interaction of curved lines with straight lines.

Details

As you look at your inspiration, think about which details are important. Be sure to strip away anything that is not central to your main idea. If you have time, or can get online, look at the work of Milton Avery. He was a painter in the early part of the twentieth century whose aim was to distill his landscapes and interior scenes down to blocks of pure color. It's not surprising that he and Mark Rothko were friends and had similar aims, but in Avery's work you can see the realistic beginnings of the scene, and thus the way he has pulled out what is most important is quite evident. There is a lot to learn from looking at art.

Take Your Time

Always take your time. This is the opposite advice from that given to you everywhere these days—whether it's work or play. And how refreshing! Making art is not a race; let go of the tension to reach the finish line. Enjoy the journey and the process, and become quietly aware of all the richness and meaningfulness around you. The design step should be taken slowly and thoughtfully, yet it is so often rushed. I feel so sad when I look at poorly designed quilts. We have all seen them—hours and hours of time have been spent on execution, with very little time spent on thinking and planning. If you want to grow and make better work, you need to slow down.

Where to Begin

Once you have collected, looked at, and thought about all the fascinating inspirations in our visual world, the next step is to choose a few views of the same subject. Don't panic! Don't get hung up on feeling that you have to choose the *absolute right* thing. You can always change your mind later—you can even choose two views and work on them both at once—but you must begin with something.

Think about the subject in the way I've been describing, and then write down your main idea. It might look something like one of these:

- The bloom on the fruit
- The sun shining through daffodils
- The pattern of geometric shapes in jumbled roofs
- The abstract pattern of wires and pumps inside a car engine

In *City of Garlic and Sapphires*, my main idea was the strange pattern of roofs seen from above (I took the photo from a clock tower), plus the distant misty countryside.

City of Garlic and Sapphires by Elizabeth Barton, 58" × 57"

Now write a short paragraph (about 100 words) expressing what it is about the main idea that captures your eye and makes you want to spend weeks making a piece about it. Pin this paragraph up on your design wall. The paragraph might read something like this:

> *I want to make a piece about sitting on the deck of my brother's house in Canada. I see a jumbled pattern of lattice fences and archways, which always remind me of him since he loves to make this kind of thing. The air is cool and I hear birds singing and twittering. I feel very relaxed since I'm a guest and have no chores! There are patterns of leaf shadows and sunlight on the decking, which is painted a soft green that is popular here. My eye is drawn to a patch of pink cosmos.*

From the paragraph I can pull out and note the following important design information:

- Deck
- Jumbled pattern of lattice fences and archways
- Cool air
- Birds twittering
- Relaxed mood
- Patterns of leaf shadows and sunlight
- Soft green
- Pink cosmos—possible focal point

Do this with your paragraph. Notice how I have included shapes, lines, values, colors, and textures in my notes. Okay, I hear you ask, how can I get twittering into my piece? Well, just think about it: You've got five design elements: shape, line, value, color, and texture. Of those, I think line would work best to show twittering. Pick up a pencil and draw a line that shows moaning—not too difficult, right? Draw a squeaking line. And now, a twittering one. Of course your twittering line might be a little different from mine, but probably not as much as you might think.

EXERCISE	Think about Your Inspiration

Use your inspiration notebook, or if you haven't got one, start one now.

1. Pick several images that inspire you or have caught your eye for one reason or another. Don't worry too much about which images; this is an exercise to get you going. You may decide to make a quilt from this inspiration, or you might not. It really doesn't matter. The more you practice using this process, the more comfortable it will become.

2. Make notes about what you like about the image.

3. Decide what the main idea is. If you were to make a quilt with this image as inspiration, what would the quilt be about?

4. Review the questions to ask yourself about the inspiration, and answer them.

5. Write a paragraph about the main idea.

Go through this exercise several times with different images.

GENERATING DESIGNS

Design Sketches

There are many ways to generate designs. I'm going to describe several of them in the next few pages and provide some exercises so you can give them all a try, but remember there are many more ways that you can manipulate sketches—and they are all so much fun! The great thing is that you can play with these possibilities anywhere. (Make boring meetings worthwhile—I have done a lot of designs while sitting through endless discussions about minutiae.) You will find that you'll be able to come up with many more ways of playing with, manipulating, and altering imagery once you've tried out a few of the exercises that follow.

Somebody in class once grumbled to me that she thought many of the following ideas would not work. What she didn't know was that they *all* work, though not *all* of the time with *all* kinds of images. I know they work because I derived many of them from looking at and seeing what painters have done, and then I've tried them out myself, or have had people in classes do them. In trying out some different possibilities, you will think of more. The idea is to loosen up and experiment—don't feel that every sketch you do has to be a perfect design. You're only using paper and pencil, so try some different ideas. Don't defeat yourself before you begin. Just give it a go, and play.

It's a good idea to work through as many of the following design sketch ideas as you can—not so much because that will give you more designs, but rather because it shows you *how* to come up with designs. It shows you the actual process of working from the original inspiration to generate design possibilities. Remember, the development of designs is *not* a critique phase. Be loose. Try to make at least a dozen designs. Sometimes I'll spend several days just dreaming up and playing with designs that I then pin up on the design wall so that I can study them over time and see which continue to interest me.

The most likely source of inspiration for an art quilt is one of your photographs—thanks to digital cameras we all have millions of them! So let's start there. Inspiration does not have to be visual, of course, but it's a good place to begin.

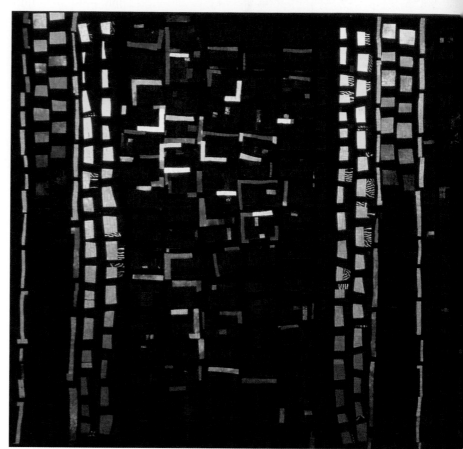

Red Shift 2 by Elizabeth Barton, 61″ × 61″

Red Shift 2 was the result of playing with the idea of a variety of squares constructed within squares using as many different red fabrics as I could find.

YOU'RE NOT ALONE

"Real artists" struggle with sketches, ideas, manipulations, and questions of "Will it work this way" or "Will it work that way" just like all of us. The only difference is that most of them have been doing it a lot longer and have often had the luxury of longer periods of time in which to practice.

Working with Photographs or Pictures
TRACING FROM THE ORIGINAL

To make a tracing of the photo or picture you have chosen, use a light table and tracing paper, or tape the original to a window and tape plain paper over the top. If the original picture has something on the back, make a photocopy of it so that the image on the back will not show through and confuse you. Don't fuss with small details. Simplify! Do not even *think* about the colors. I usually print my photographs out on a sheet of plain white paper. You don't have to print them very large because you don't want those distracting little details. Then I use a light table to sketch them onto tracing paper.

Below is an example of an original photo, the sketch I made from it, and the resulting quilt.

Edging Into Line by
Elizabeth Barton, 22″ × 46″

After you have the sketch, make several copies of it. You will use each of these in a different way to create more designs. Put the original up on the wall. Mount it on construction paper if you have it. I like mounting a sketch onto black construction paper, which helps to isolate it from the other sketches and also helps me to think about it as a work of art on its own. Make your designs bold and black so they can be seen easily when you stand back from the design wall.

CROPPING

To make cropping tools, either cut an old picture mat into two L-shaped pieces, or cut L-shaped pieces from black paper or card stock.

Picture mat

Cut picture mat in half.

The L shapes (your cropping tools) allow you to discover interesting little compositions within larger images. Let your intuition and curiosity take over here. In photos of art, often it is the detail shots that are more striking than the whole image. Why can a detail be stronger than the whole piece? One big reason is that a detail has some mystery to it; we have to work to figure out the whole picture, and that keeps us involved with a piece. Also, the detail focuses in closely on just one thing so there is nothing to distract us and take us off message. And in a detail, we can often see just a few large, interesting shapes (remember Milton Avery's work that I suggested earlier you might like to see, page 12) or just a few elegant lines.

When you are working on an idea for a quilt design, copy and enlarge these cropped areas, but don't make them any larger than an ordinary sheet of copier paper. A design sketch does not need to be the same size as the actual quilt you will make based on it. There's a lot more room for creativity and serendipity as you build the quilt on the design wall if your sketch is fairly small.

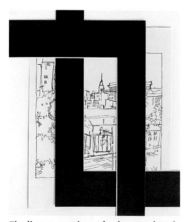

Finding a section of a larger sketch

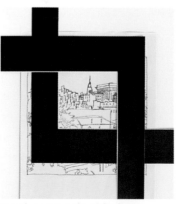

Another example of finding a section of a larger sketch

Lendal Bridge by Elizabeth Barton, 60″ × 62″

While you might enlarge and use a crop to create a quilt, another good way to use crops is to multiply them. I remember one student who made a wonderful quilt from a crop of a drawing of a cow. The workshop was in a small country town and there was a dairy farm next door. She went over with her camera and took several pictures of cows, with their beautiful, bold, black and white markings. She traced a sketch and cropped down to the most interesting cow head she could find. The cow's markings formed an intriguing pattern—especially when interpreted in fuchsia, lime green, yellow, and black!

Museum St. by Elizabeth Barton, 35″ × 54″

I took a photo of *Lendal Bridge*, used my cropping tools, found a section I really liked, and made *Museum St.* from that section.

Semmerwater by Elizabeth Barton, 54″ × 37″

In this piece, the house and chimney shapes are repeated with changes in value and color, with positive and negative space, and with horizontal orientation.

Five Mills Rampant by Elizabeth Barton, 57″ × 25″

Photo by Karen J. Hamrick

Five repeats in a row

EXERCISE Discovering Interesting Crops

1. Pick up a book or magazine with large photos and play with the L-shaped cropping tools: See if you can find interesting details that might actually be stronger than the original piece.

2. Now, trace one of the photographs you selected in the previous exercise on thinking about your inspiration. Be sure to simplify the design.

3. Move the cropping tools around on a copy of the traced, simplified design to discover interesting little compositions. Let your intuition and curiosity take over here.

EXERCISE Crops Multiplied

Take one small detail that you have discovered in the previous cropping exercise (at left) and repeat it in a four-patch. Use no more than five bold shapes. Don't think about color yet! That's coming in Choosing a Color Scheme (page 63). You could also experiment with a nine-patch or a row or column if the traditional four-patch does not look good.

DESIGNING ON A GRID

I like using a grid as a background because it helps to anchor a piece. I've noticed that it is not only quilters but many artists who love grids. Chuck Close often grids his work. Richard Diebenkorn transforms the local landscape into loose, irregular grids in his Ocean Park Series. Bridget Riley organizes her shapes into vertical grids with diagonal lines. There are many more examples. If you start to collect grid ideas, you'll soon have a nice little store of them that you can use when you need them. The number of quilters who have used a grid is vast. Take an hour or so to research all the different ways grids have been used, and then you can adapt many of these ideas for your own quilt designs. Grids also abound everywhere in our environment—a walk down the street will reveal at least half a dozen examples.

The grid can be quite geometric, with true horizontal and vertical lines and all squares the same, or very relaxed, with lines drawn at any angle.

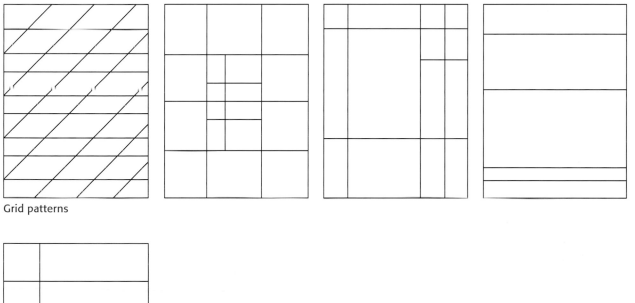

Grid patterns

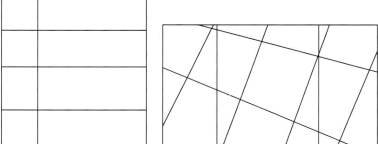

Grids observed while walking down the street

Using Grids

1. Draw a grid, any grid!

2. Draw one or two simple shapes from one of your sketches within the confines of the grid.

3. Next, try superimposing a cropped section from a sketch on top of a grid. To do this, choose a *dominant shape* from the sketch, such as a leaf shape, and superimpose it in different sizes on the patchwork background in either a loose or rigid pattern. Another possibility would be to overlay the shapes with the same shape, but just in outline, as in a stitched outline. You can make several of these sketches, some with quite rigid shapes, some with floating ones. See how many ideas you can come up with.

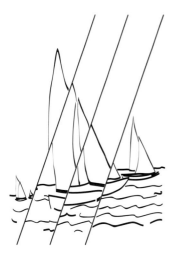

Four possible ways to arrange shapes on top of grids

SLICE AND REARRANGE

Another way to come up with design ideas is to cut design sketches into sections and rearrange them. Think about all the different ways you can do this. I'm deliberately not giving too much specific information about the size, shape, or number of sections because I don't want you to limit yourself.

I do want to give you this one specific example: Notice how one sketch sliced diagonally and shifted slightly gives a sense of movement.

Sailboat sliced diagonally to give sense of forward movement and choppy water

Bicycle girl sliced horizontally, giving impression of making bike jump

Do the following exercises and see what you come up with.

| EXERCISE | ## Cut, Combine, Rearrange |

1. Take at least two copies of a sketch, cut them into sections, and rearrange them. Try different shapes and numbers of cuts. Be sure to try using more than two copies of a sketch to see how you can repeat as you rearrange. Sections can be horizontal, vertical, diagonal, curved, spiky—whatever you wish!

2. Cut at least one sketch on the diagonal, and see how shifting it changes the feeling.

POSITIVE AND NEGATIVE SHAPES

Negative shapes are at least as important as positive ones. A positive shape is generally an object. If we look at a teapot, the positive shape is the pot itself and the negative shape is all the space around the teapot. In an interesting piece, the negative shapes will be as fascinating as the positive ones. Teapots are good examples because they not only hold the promise of a nice cup of tea but also have a lot of ins and outs and curly bits, so the negative shape around them also has ins and outs and curly bits. And there's nothing better to include in your piece than ins and outs and curly bits! Look at the skies in some of my nighttime street quilts and you can see how I've tried to make the shape of the night sky just as interesting as the shapes of the old houses. This isn't just chance, it's deliberate.

Pick up an art book or visit your local gallery and examine how artists use negative shapes to make their work more compelling.

Shambles, November by Elizabeth Barton, 38" × 70"

Petergate by Elizabeth Barton, 37″ × 45″

Peckett's Yard by Elizabeth Barton, 50″ × 58″

EXERCISE Positive and Negative Shapes

Now it's your turn!

1. Choose a shape from one of your sketches, either large or small, but it should be an interesting one. It's easier to develop an interesting negative shape from an interesting positive one—think about the teapot!

2. Draw a grid of any kind. Even just vertical or horizontal lines will work beautifully. The reason for the grid is simply to organize the shapes and give some depth to the design. If you'd like to try without one, feel free to do so.

3. Find a piece of colored paper. Any color will do; it is just to give you a different value from white so that you can see the positives and the negatives clearly.

4. Trace or sketch the shape you have chosen. Cut it out carefully without cutting into the background. Now you have two shapes. One is the positive shape that you cut out. The other is the background with the hole where the positive shape was—this is the negative shape.

5. Play with these shapes, repeating them or overlapping them as in the examples below. Take your time. Have fun.

Nine-patch positive/negative circle in square

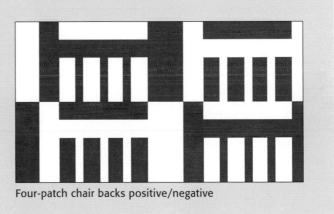

Four-patch chair backs positive/negative

FAVORITE SHAPES

It's funny how people have favorite shapes. There's probably a lot we can learn about personality from this! Take a look at the following examples, and then try it yourself with the exercise on page 25 and some of your sketches.

Design using only circles, based on flowerpots, table, and chairs on my deck

You don't have to be completely rigid about this—if you need a straight line or something else here or there, feel free.

Photo by Karen J. Hamrick

Strength of Quiet Windows by Elizabeth Barton, 41″ × 55″

This quilt is made just from rectangles.

Yellow Mountain by Elizabeth Barton, 55″ × 36″

This quilt is made primarily from triangles.

Looking Out the Back by Elizabeth Barton, 56" × 27"

This quilt uses mainly rhomboid and trapezoid shapes.

<table>
<tr><td>EXERCISE</td><td></td></tr>
</table>

EXERCISE Using Your Favorite Shape

Choose your favorite shape—square, triangle, circle, or anything else—and redraw one of your designs using only that shape. Make different sizes of the shape. You can stretch it or rotate it. Be loose! Have fun!

FREEHAND DRAWING

Sketching freehand helps you learn what is important and what is not important, and usually there's a lot more unimportant stuff. For example, if you have photograph of a building with a lot of windows, you really don't need to include them all in your design—you can just hint at them. You can get the essence across with just a few symbols, just as teenage (or not) texters do. If you were the architect of a building, obviously you'd want to indicate just how many windows the building has and where exactly they are located, but if you're an artist wanting to give just a general sense of a cityscape with interlocking jigsaw-like shapes, it's the *interlocking* that is more important, not how many dots or squares are on the shapes.

St. Ives by Elizabeth Barton, 62" × 34"

Notice how the windows in the very light-colored house at the front are not completely spelled out; I've made each one a little different, too, with a different reflection of light.

EXERCISE Freehand Drawing

Take one of your design sketches, look at it carefully for one minute, put it away, and redraw it freehand. This will force you to simplify. What can you leave out? Which bits are not really interesting? If there's something you don't remember, it probably isn't important.

REPETITION OF ELEMENTS

Remember that your original inspiration is just a starting point. A good way to create a new design is to use the main visual theme of your inspiration and create variations of it. Perhaps you have a house, a tree, and a person. A variation could be two houses, three trees, and one person. If you had a pattern of three stripes alternating in colors, you could reverse the order or double a color. Many landscape artists re-create landscapes similar to those they've already painted, but they might add more trees or vary the distance between them.

One of my first quilts included window shapes (a rectangle with a narrow strip added to each side). On the next quilt in the series I simply doubled the strips added to each side. By the time I made *Aiming High* (at right), the thirteenth quilt in the series, I was not only doubling side pieces but repeating the original window idea in several different sizes within the quilt.

Using Ideas from Others

Picasso is reputed to have said that mediocre artists copy ideas but good artists steal them! Now what he meant was *not* that you'd copy art that someone else had made, but rather you'd analyze an idea, or a way of showing something, then you'd take that process, manipulation, or image, develop it, and make it your own. For example, Nancy Crow (www.nancycrow.com) took from Anna Williams the idea that "lines do not have to be straight" and ran with it—far and wide! Look at how her work changed from the beautiful but complex and rigid early quilts to the vast outpouring of new pieces once she had observed, and then made her own, that one idea of disregarding straight lines, symmetry, matching, precision, and so on. Actually, she wasn't the first artist to eschew the straight line. Friedensreich Hundertwasser in Austria hated straight lines; he actually thought they were evil! He designed some striking buildings that have soft, flowing, natural lines, and he made a lot of paintings and sketches showing how he had developed his ideas.

For my own work, I saw one painter gradate the sky color vertically instead of horizontally. I really liked the vertical, upright strength that gave to the landscape, so I used that idea in a couple of my quilts.

Aiming High by Elizabeth Barton, 40″ × 60″

In *Aiming High* I used the same idea of square-within-a-square in a number of different ways.

Headland House by Elizabeth Barton, 60″ × 66″

As another example, why not use a technique from weaving? I've seen quilts in which this has been done quite effectively: Two designs were cut into strips and woven together. It also works well with two pieces of interesting surface-designed fabric. Susan Brandeis has made several superb quilts based on this idea (www.sefea.us > Artists > Susan Brandeis > View Artwork).

Bold designs, such as a large circle in a square, work best with this manipulation. Larry Schulte has made some beautiful paper collages this way (www.larryschulte.com > Woven Photographs).

You can also go a step further and use cropping tools on the woven piece to see if you can find something worth developing.

EXERCISE Make It Your Own

Okay, so what could you use? And using means *making your own*, not slavishly copying.

- Pull out some pictures of your favorite art quilts. Write down what you particularly like about the work, and then take one of your previous sketches and redo it, adding in some of the features you really like. For example, if you really like the way a person cut an image into three vertical strips and made three quilts— that would be something to try with an image of a quilt you've already made. Picasso was intrigued by the way Braque tried to paint pictures based on the constant fluctuation of vision. He took the idea and made it his own by developing it further and further. Think about ways different artists might have interpreted your theme or image. What can you learn from them?

- Artist Richmond Burton likes to manipulate ideas. He suggests the following techniques: splattering, rearranging, reconfiguring, reanimating, fragmenting, fracturing, dissecting, devastating. See if you can come up with words like these for yourself and then try them out on your first traced image. Above all, make a lot! Do not be satisfied with the first sketch!

- Repeat some or all of these exercises with a second picture if you have time. Remember, you want a lot of ideas to choose from.

Music as a Design Source

Music has been and is a source of design inspiration for many artists. It can evoke emotions, textures, rhythms, shapes, and more. It can suggest colors and lines.

Vision by Elizabeth Barton, 45″ × 63″

I made this piece after listening to Hildegard von Bingen's *Vision* music.

Geoff's Shed by Elizabeth Barton, 34″ × 49″

I made the fabric for this quilt by doodling with a syringe full of dye.

Listen to a favorite piece of music, and as you listen, draw or doodle. You can draw the emotions, the rhythms, the shapes that come to mind. Don't forget to vary the quality of the lines and think about different textures, too. What shapes come to mind as you listen? What contrast of values? What color is a Viennese waltz? What lines suggest a nocturne? Is the *1812 Overture* bright red and black or is it green and blue? Remember, you have just five elements: shape, line, value, color, texture. So you can ask yourself fairly specific questions, as I have demonstrated. And such questions will soon get the creative juices flowing!

Your sketch can be abstract, based on the rhythm or mood of the piece, or realistic if the piece makes you think of something concrete like moonlight, drums, or waving palm trees. There are no right or wrong responses. Take a risk. You have to be prepared to take risks and make mistakes if you want to progress; if you wait for the perfect right answer, you'll be waiting a long, long time.

Words as a Design Source

Just as with music, words can be a source of inspiration. Whether it is poetry or just individual words, there is no end to the inspiration you can find in words.

EXERCISE Word Games

This is fun … so much fun it's almost a parlor game. Get out a pencil and paper. You can enroll anyone passing by: kids, friends, even spouses. Anyone can do it.

1. Write down on a piece of scratch paper ten verbs. Use verbs instead of nouns because it's harder to be literal with a verb. With a noun like *flower* or *pizza* you might be tempted just to draw the object. Also, verbs are much more active and dynamic.

2. Draw a rectangle on your design paper. Draw another rectangle within the first one. Anywhere.

3. In each space put marks or shapes corresponding to two of the verbs. For example, if you chose the verb *inject*, you could draw a mark like a simplified syringe.

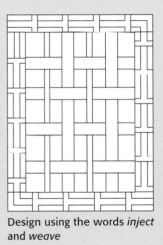

Design using the words *inject* and *weave*

4. Try this with columns—I've drawn five of similar size but you choose the number and relative widths.

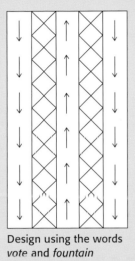

Design using the words *vote* and *fountain*

5. Repeat Step 3 using only one mark or symbol, but divide the rectangle into three and draw the mark a different size in each space, for example, small ones in one space, larger ones in another, one giant one in the third space.

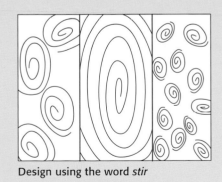

Design using the word *stir*

Here's a variation: Make up three rules for yourself. The first one should specify the way the rectangle (the first four lines of your composition) is divided up; the second one should relate to how many of the verbs you will use. The third one should indicate size and placement of the marks. See how creative you can be! There are endless possibilities with this formula. This is fun to play with when you are stuck in a waiting room or while on hold on the telephone.

POETRY

Poetry is both meaning and sound. You can respond to either. Look up your favorite poems or use these links to poems that could inspire several quilts:

- "The Highwayman" by Alfred Noyes has a driving rhythm and a great story; it's dramatic and you can picture the dark moor at night and hear the beat of the horse's hooves. (www.potw.org > Past Poem Archive by Title and First Line > Highwayman, The)

- "Poem in October" by Dylan Thomas has a lot of sounds, smells, and kinesthetic feelings as well as visual imagery. You can extract any of these in realistic or abstract form. (www.poetryfoundation.org > Search: Poem in October)

- The phrase "wide water" occurs in the Wallace Stevens poem "Sunday Morning" (www.poemhunter.com > Search: Sunday Morning). It makes me think of a quilt that is about water and space and light (below).

Farne Islands by Elizabeth Barton, 60″ × 47″

Farne Islands was inspired by a boat ride out to some small islands that are now a bird sanctuary. I was fascinated by the changing surface of the water, at times roiling and bubbling, or making sinuous patterns, or splashing up against the rocks. It was a wonderful day.

Wrap-Up

Put all your sketches up on the design wall, grouping together those that relate to a specific theme. Remember the main idea or theme is what you want a piece to convey. It does not have to be anything enormously significant, but having a theme will help you to decide the quality of the basic design elements of shape, line, color, value, texture, and direction when you are beginning to make the actual piece. It is helpful to write the main idea or theme on the drawing.

For the next few days, keep looking at the designs. If one starts to look really boring, move it down to a reject corner. You may still mine these for ideas, but they are not first runners. The good ones stay. On to the next step!

Step 2:
Size, Shape, and Structure

This chapter covers how to choose the size, shape, and structure that will best fit your idea. As with designing a house, you decide how big it will be. Then you decide what kind of a footprint and, finally, how the rooms will fit together and work as a whole. You can't build a house without first making these decisions, and it's difficult to make a good quilt without giving the same factors considerable thought—though there is always room for a few adjustments at the end.

Size and Shape

After you have the main idea or theme for your quilt, the next step is to get a rough idea of the shape and size you want the quilt to be, but don't lock yourself into a precise size just yet. Most quilts are rectangular or square—they have four outside edges. Those four edges are the first four lines in the composition and are very important. If you draw four short ones of equal length you have a small square. Draw four long edges of equal length and you have a large square. Two shorter sides and two longer sides give you a rectangle. You have to decide roughly how far apart these four lines should be and what ratio their lengths should be to each other. Make that decision based on your theme.

In *The Red Gate* (at right), I wanted the viewer to get a sense of being able to open the gate or go up the old steps, so it needed to be about the size of a person for that to happen.

The Red Gate by Elizabeth Barton, 39″ × 63″

If you want to show an intimate scene, a smaller size is usually more appropriate. To see a small piece, the viewer comes close and focuses in on the work. If your piece is about the breadth of the prairies, a wide rectangle would support that idea well. If your theme is the towering coastal pines and spruces in British Columbia, you want a tall rectangle.

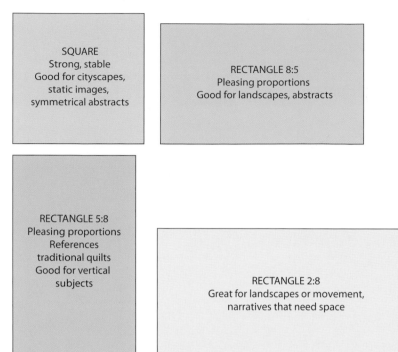

SQUARE
Strong, stable
Good for cityscapes, static images, symmetrical abstracts

RECTANGLE 8:5
Pleasing proportions
Good for landscapes, abstracts

RECTANGLE 5:8
Pleasing proportions
References traditional quilts
Good for vertical subjects

RECTANGLE 2:8
Great for landscapes or movement, narratives that need space

Possible outlines

People often make quilts about doorways, openings, and entrances to a strange or mystical space—if you do, support that idea by making the quilt the size of a doorway.

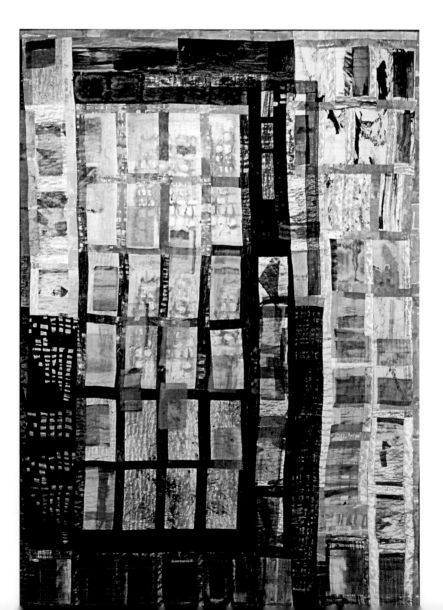

Reflections by Elizabeth Barton,
43″ × 63″

Rectangular doorway quilt

If your theme is an intricate mathematical idea or variation on an abstract symbol, then a balanced square of medium size would be a good neutral shape leading to no specific expectations.

After you've determined your main idea and thought it through, place four skinny lengths of fabric or string on the design wall to outline the shape of the quilt-to-be (see my design wall with pinned-up sketches, page 6). This process is similar to that of a painter choosing the size of her canvas. As a quiltmaker, you have an advantage in that you can always add (or subtract) an inch or two, or more, to either the height or width of the piece during the process.

Tip When you do commission work, you may have to make the size and shape of the quilt fit a specific space. This was the case with a quilt I made for a quarter-moon-shaped space at Hartsfield Atlanta Airport.

Wheels by Elizabeth Barton, 96″ × 190″

If you're working on a series of quilts, being able to envisage the gallery wall with a row of small squares, or large squares, or tall skinny rectangles, or whatever will work best for you, is both really helpful in your planning and highly motivating.

Structure

It's best to have an overall plan, structure, or pattern scheme for a composition. Another name for this is the "hidden order"—you don't see it at first, but it is the way in which the main elements are organized. Some people conceive of it as being an overall shape that underlies and supports all the different shapes and lines that make up the quilt. Think of the underlying structure as being like a skeleton or the main support beams framing a house. Having a clear design structure provides unity and pulls the design together, and unity depends upon organization.

When trying to learn about structure in quilts, it's helpful to see how others have used it. Look at quilts that you instinctively know are successful, such as quilts by major artists who have won much acclaim, and see if you can figure out what the underlying structural organization is. Many traditional quilts have a clear, strong structure. Repeated blocks obviously have a grid structure; Lone Star quilts have a radiating basic format; patterns such as Chinese Coins have a strong vertical structure; Drunkard's Path and Irish Chain designs embody strong diagonal lines, basic X shapes that hold the pieces together.

In contemporary quilts, it is obvious that some artists plan their pieces on a grid, while others have a more linear approach (either horizontal or vertical). Some choose a shape such as a letter, while others divide up the space into different sections, either geometric or organic.

Full Circle by Elizabeth Barton, two pieces, each 50″ × 80″

This quilt is organized by an overall O or circular shape.

See if you can spot these structures when you look at the quilts. Carol Taylor and Dominie Nash have clear structures in their work (www.caroltaylorquilts.com; www.dominienash.com). Squint at the quilts and figure out what the plan was. Decide what kind of structure appeals to you. Take a look at possible design structures I describe, and then go back to your own sketches. Can you see which ones you have naturally organized in a structure? Notice how the ones with such a structure have more strength and completeness. See if there are improvements you can make using a clear structure.

Designing Structures

Most people choose a structure intuitively and may not specifically think about it, but it's helpful to be able to think analytically and discuss a design and its structure. When a quilt is not going as you envisioned, structure is the first thing to check. Furthermore, the ways of organizing items in a two-dimensional shape of reasonable size are fairly limited, as you can see in the next five pages, so you don't have to hunt around through millions of possibilities.

There are different ways of categorizing different design structures. Once you know the kind of underlying shape or organization that appeals to you, you can use it many times, like a favorite recipe. Opposing diagonal lines are one of my favorite underlying structures to use because they have a great deal of energy and excitement. However, many people prefer a calmer, horizontal structure, such as that in a seascape or landscape, or a basic grid because of its stability and familiarity. Any structure is fine—as long as there *is* a structure: We all need good bones!

GRID STRUCTURES

A grid structure is strong and beautiful as well as flexible—there are many different grids you can choose from (pages 19 and 20).

LINEAR STRUCTURES

Linear structures can be horizontal, vertical, diagonal, or a combination.

Remembered Lines by Elizabeth Barton, 69″ × 41″

I chose a linear design structure because linear structures are stable and solid, traditional and defined. I wanted to give the impression of a building that had stood the test of time, and I was obviously influenced by the external timbers seen on medieval buildings and the way old houses develop curves. These irregularities and shifts away from purely straight vertical lines add variety. As you can see I've definitely shimmied and wobbled the lines in this piece. The basically vertical structure is significant in unifying the design; it is the details that add the variety. Both are important in making an interesting and satisfying piece.

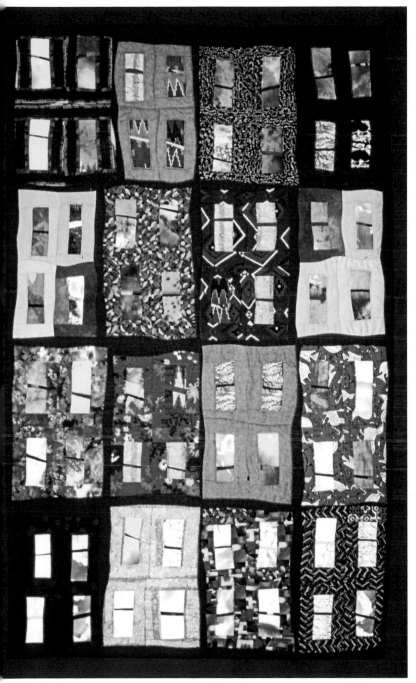

Jazz City by Elizabeth Barton, 46″ × 72″

This quilt is organized by a grid.

Hours 1pm by Elizabeth Barton, 37″ × 38″

Diagonal structure

Kite by Elizabeth Barton, 40″ × 45″

Diagonal structure

Stanley by Elizabeth Barton, 44″ × 60″

Horizontal structure

Chimney Tops by Elizabeth Barton, 50″ × 40″

In *Chimney Tops*, the repetition of the diagonal lines forms the principal organizing structure. I used diagonal lines because they are dynamic, having a lot of thrust and energy. In fact, they have so much energy and direction that it's important not to have all the diagonals going in one direction. I wanted to convey the upward-reaching feeling of these rooftops, but I also wanted them to appear stable and sheltering.

King's Square by Elizabeth Barton, 42" × 67"

Diagonal structure

Lightfall by Elizabeth Barton, 35" × 76"

Vertical structure

LETTER-SHAPED STRUCTURES

The structure can be shaped like the letters U, S, L, T, or O. For example, *Pump Court* (page 9) is based on an inverted U, *Lendal Bridge* (page 17) has an S-shaped structure, *Reflections* (page 32) has an L-shaped basis to it, and *Peckett's Yard* (page 22) has a T structure. You can choose to work from a geometric idea or think of a letter; either way it will work. The letter O is a circular structure, while T and L have a vertical basis—just find the way that is most natural for you to think about it.

Age Cannot Wither by Elizabeth Barton, 62″ × 84″

Battersea by Elizabeth Barton, 18″ × 24″

The main structural lines radiate out from the vanishing point at the end of the street. The clear structure helps to unify the piece. The choice of a radiating design helps to give a sense of walking down that street, especially since this quilt is quite large. I chose this size and organization of shapes because I wanted it to feel as if you were there, looking down the medieval street on a late winter afternoon. I hoped the viewer would feel like Alice in *Through the Looking Glass*, with a sense of being able to simply step into the old street the way Alice stepped through the mirror.

In *Battersea*, the main shapes of the building are arranged into a triangle. The Battersea Power Station actually has four main chimneys, but I was lucky enough to get a photograph (taken from an idyllic ride down the Thames River on a barge) that showed just three chimneys. I used a triangular design structure because of what I felt about the power station: a huge and massive building made of stone, which has been standing by the river for well over a century. The triangle shape is strong, stable, and long-lasting. Think of the pyramids. The art deco design of the power station, its location, the material from which it is made, and the immensity of it all are conveyed by the use of that design structure.

Oculus by Elizabeth Barton, 71″ × 48″

The structure of this quilt goes around a point.

GEOMETRIC-SHAPED STRUCTURES

Full Circle (page 34) has a circular structure.

Cathedral by Elizabeth Barton, 42″ × 58″

This quilt has a triangular structure.

Wrap-Up

A thoughtfully selected structure will help support your main idea and provide the bones for strong and clear organization—you don't want to make a quilt that rambles along like an old house that has had bits added on over the centuries. The structure of the design should make visual sense. I have seen jumbled-up quilts upon which, sadly, the maker has lavished much time and effort. All the beads in the world won't transform a poorly structured design into something elegant and meaningful.

Another way to think about underlying structure is in terms of music. A well-written piece of music is made up of many different sounds organized in such a way as to create a mood, tell a story, describe a scene, or explore variations on an intriguing sequence of notes. But if the notes and chords are disorganized, you have cacophony. Avoid creating visual cacophony in your quilts! Just as in music, the different notes in visual art should be organized with the intent to interest the viewer and convey a feeling or idea. People do not like to feel confused, whether the stimulus is aural or visual. They will stop listening or stop looking.

A quick surf around the Internet will reveal plenty of cacophonous quilts, and you can learn from them. When you see an awkward quilt, don't just pass it by but see if you can figure out what's wrong (Evaluating a Design, page 75). The more practice you get at critiquing, the stronger your own designs will be.

Step 3:
Depth and Space

Depth, space, and the placement of the basic elements of shape and line (the fabric pieces and the stitching) have a significant effect on the overall success of the piece.

Deep or Shallow?

The first thing to decide is whether you want a sense of depth in your quilt. What I mean by this is do you want your quilt to have a three-dimensional illusion, as if the shapes are in a space having depth? Or do you want to compress the space and have a totally two-dimensional look to the piece? It's the difference between looking into a lit window at the room beyond or even through a door at the back of that room to another one (as Vermeer often did), and looking at a window and having all the things inside the window appear to be right up against the glass.

Either of these approaches to depth is absolutely fine; there's no right or wrong. You need to decide what is best for the quilt. Traditional quilt patterns and most (but definitely not all) abstract work tend to be in rather shallow space; more representational (landscape or cityscape) work tends to use deeper space.

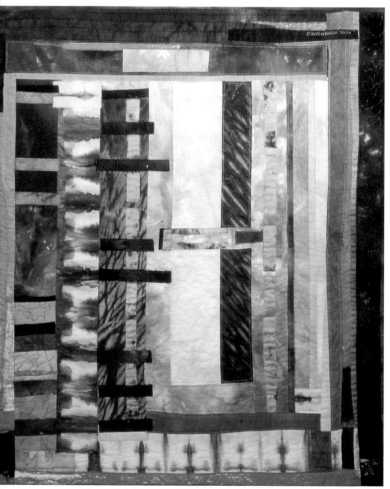

On the Latch by Elizabeth Barton, 34″ × 40″

While this quilt was about a specific idea and a doorway, I wanted it to be two-dimensional and abstract, indicating a very shallow depth of space.

Milltown Morning by Elizabeth Barton, 54″ × 34″

Depth was necessary for this quilt about a small town in the moorland of Yorkshire because I wanted to emphasize its setting, with the vast moors extending beyond; there is a tremendous sense of the space around one in these small, moorland mill towns.

Devices for Creating the Illusion of Depth

If you decide you want deeper space, then you will use one or more (usually more) of the devices available for creating an illusion of depth. The main strategies are overlapping, color, contrast, texture, size, and placement.

OVERLAPPING

Overlapping is one of the most effective and most used ways of indicating depth. It simply means that you place one thing over another. If you have a mountain in a design, overlap it with a tree. Our brains are hardwired to decipher that image to indicate that the tree is in front of the mountain. We do not make the mistake of thinking that the mountain has a tree-shaped hole in it, through which we can see a distant (and probably giant) tree. There are other reasons for overlapping shapes, too—for one thing, it helps to clump them together, which unifies the design.

COLOR

As you look into the distance, colors change. This happens because you are looking through the atmosphere and, alas, it is often dirty or soggy with humidity, making distant things seem grayer or bluer than they really are. Any classic photo of the Smoky Mountains shows them becoming a paler and paler blue-gray the further they are away from you. The "smoke," of course, is the moisture in the air from all the trees. This phenomenon is often called "aerial perspective." So if you make a quilt with distant mountains, hills, forests, or even buildings, using a soft, smoky, gray-blue fabric for them will make them look a lot further away. Don't make the mistake of choosing some nice pink and yellow "rock" fabric.

Edge of Light by Elizabeth Barton, 41″ × 24″

In *Edge of Light*, depth is indicated by overlapping one row of houses over another.

Photo by Karen J. Hamrick

Overlook by Elizabeth Barton, 54″ × 40″

Notice that the distant hills are indicated in cooler, softer, grayer colors than the nearby trees and bushes.

CONTRAST

As you look into the distance, there's a lot less contrast in values. Nearby, bright lights next to the dark darks are much more distinct than the distant soft medium-light gray against a soft medium gray. Because you can see the higher contrast so clearly, your brain says, "Aha! That means those objects are closer to me." Don't use values that differ greatly next to each other in the part of the quilt you want to be the background; instead, gradate the values gently in the desired direction.

Endless City by Elizabeth Barton, 35″ × 50″

The contrast in values diminishes considerably as the buildings get further away from the viewer.

TEXTURE

If you look into the distance, you'll see that the surface pattern (whether it's leaves on a tree or bricks on a building or features on a face) becomes much less distinct. In fact, most distant things are a soft blur to all but the most eagle-eyed! And, of course, for some of us more mature folk, the soft blur comes ever nearer.

The Gatehouse by Elizabeth Barton, 37″ × 25″

In *The Gatehouse*, the distant shapes have far less texture and detail than the ones in the foreground. This creates a sense of depth.

SIZE

There's the old story of the little boy at the airport waiting for his first flight, asking, "Grandma, when will they shrink us?" The further away things are, the smaller they seem, and he saw those tiny planes in the sky and figured the passengers had to be pretty small too! So if you want to create an illusion of depth, be sure the trees get smaller as they go into the distance. Even if you're making a quilt about, say, tumbling blocks floating off into the distance, the ones furthest back should be smaller, and have less texture and contrast as described above.

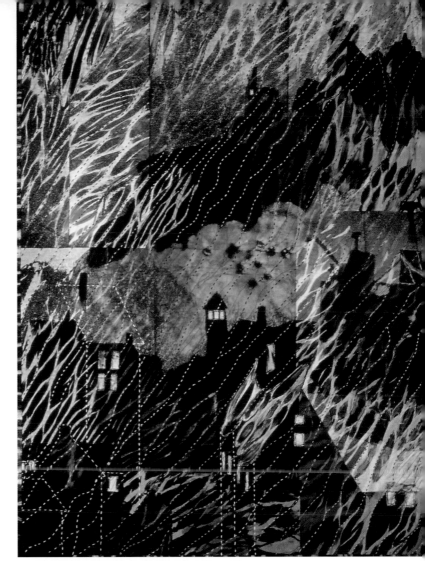

Botallack Mine by Elizabeth Barton, 28″ × 39″

Notice how the houses get smaller and less distinct as they recede in the distance.

PLACEMENT

In Western art we have the convention that the further away something is from us, the higher up the picture plane it tends to be. I think this is because we simply cannot see something at ground level in the distance. The only place we can see things right at ground level (for the most part) is right by our feet. You can use this convention to indicate depth: Move things up in the design if you want to suggest that they are further away.

Hostler's Row by Elizabeth Barton, 40″ × 27″

In addition to using all the techniques mentioned to achieve a sense of depth, I placed houses higher up to suggest they are further away.

Perspective

A lot of people have said to me, "I can't do depth because I can't draw in perspective." Don't worry!

There are a lot of ways of indicating depth, including those I have just described, and none of them require any special knowledge; in fact, many, many artists never bother with perspective at all. Accurate perspective is much more necessary for precise architectural drawings than for art. Furthermore, drawing in perspective is a skill and, like many skills, is not a natural talent but rather something the person has learned. It's also not a particularly difficult or complicated skill, and there are many books that simplify it. Also, drawing in perspective tends to make a design much more rigid and less painterly. So I'm actually not a big fan of obsessively correct, architectural-style work. However, there are a few pointers worth remembering, as follows.

SIMPLE PERSPECTIVE GUIDELINES

The first thing to know about perspective is that verticals are *always* vertical. That's easy to remember—any buildings you have will always have their vertical lines straight up and down, aligned with the sides of the quilt.

If you're working on a representational piece, I find it's always helpful to begin with a horizon line. The horizon line is the line where sea or land meets the sky. It's the farthest end of the horizontal plane upon which you are standing.

It's good to place the horizon somewhat above or below the exact middle of the quilt. Designs that are chopped exactly in two—unless there is a good reason—aren't as interesting as designs with varying proportions for different sections of the piece. It's the old Mother Bear, Father Bear, and Baby Bear thing—*variety*. Draw the horizon line high or higher, low or lower, depending on your theme. The horizon line is generally on a level with our eyes as we look at a landscape.

The placement of the *horizon* line affects the angle of the *horizontal* lines in the buildings. All the horizontal lines of a building facing away from a viewer, whether it's the roof (if it's flat), the window ledges, or the line where the building meets the street, go from where they start on the sketch at the point nearest to you, the viewer, out toward the horizon line. Therefore, a line from a point on the building that is above you will go downward toward the horizon line. A line from a point on the building that is below your eye level will go upward toward the horizon line. Horizontal lines facing you on buildings should be completely horizontal, parallel to the horizon line.

Perspective can get a lot more complicated if you get into two-point perspective (two points on the horizon line) as opposed to one (as described above). But just knowing that verticals are vertical and horizontals head toward the point where they vanish on the horizon will keep you largely on track.

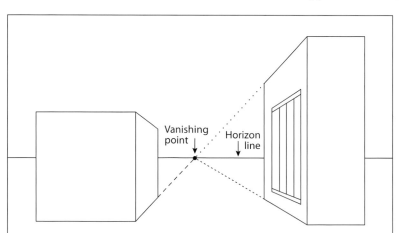

Simple one-point perspective

A New Day by Elizabeth Barton, 55" × 26"

I calculated most of the angles in this quilt using a protractor.

Perspective is simply a methodical way of showing the three-dimensionality and depth of objects in a two-dimensional framework (such as that of a painting or a wallhanging) by the way you draw (or cut) the vertical and horizontal lines of the structures you are describing. In one-point perspective, all the horizontal lines radiate from one point on the horizon, and in two-point perspective from two points (as if you are standing at the intersection of two roads and you can see both sides of a building and therefore two points on the horizon).

For issues of perspective beyond that, I suggest you do something quite different and much easier. If you have a photograph of rooftops and you wish to make sure that the rhomboid and quadrilateral roof shapes are correct in your quilt, then measure the angles. Buy yourself a protractor (page 63)—they're widely available anywhere school supplies are sold. Simply measure the angle of the rooftop in the photograph or sketch, and reproduce that same angle on the fabric when you draw the roof shape. I'll address this technique further in Construction (pages 102–104).

Focal Point or Focal Area

The focal point helps to focus viewers onto the key to the quilt. It helps them see what the quilt is about. It is the center of attention, the main subject. Like the main character in a film, or the lead tenor in an opera, the focal point emphasizes the reason for the work of art. While a focal point is not strictly necessary, for most pieces it is useful. You might not want one if your quilt is about the beauty of an abstract pattern or ripples in a desert, but even with these subjects you'll find that a person looking at the quilt will focus in on any stitching that is a little irregular. It is human nature to look for those little differences, and the artist can exploit that.

HOW LARGE CAN THE FOCAL POINT OR AREA BE?

The focal point or focal area can be fairly small, or it could also be as large as one-third of the design. The rest of the design supports the focal point. Think again about the lead tenor: He should be commanding, in charge, on stage a lot but not necessarily all the time. He shouldn't be singing every note in the whole opera. We would get bored if the whole thing were just one character and, moreover, he'd be worn out by the end of the first act!

WHERE SHOULD THE FOCAL POINT BE?

Except in unusual circumstances, it's best to place the focal point near, but not exactly at, the center of the design. It should be near the middle because that's where the viewer expects to look for it and also because it can command the quilt from that point. It's usually best not to put it slap bang right in the middle because that makes the design much more static—all the force lines go with equal strength to the middle and out. However, if you wished to make a point about feeling targeted or being at a static point, you could place the focal point in the center.

Likewise, it is best not to place the focal point right on the edge of a quilt; everyone would look at that area and disregard the rest of the piece. The only time you might want to do that is if you are making a point about feelings of marginalization or something similar.

DRAWING ATTENTION TO THE FOCAL POINT

There are many ways to make the focal point attractive, eye-catching, and important. The chief way is by creating *contrast* using the elements of design (shapes, lines, values, colors, and textures). Each design element provides different opportunities for contrast.

Shape

Using different shapes is one way to make a focal point stand out. In the midst of a field of circles, a triangle would look very different; your eyes would go to it straight away. A large circle in the middle of many small ones will capture your attention. The same holds true if you reverse that—you will see the small circle in the middle of many large ones, perhaps not quite so quickly, but you will spot it.

Midwinter by Elizabeth Barton, 44″ × 26″

In *Midwinter*, the lonely little barns are the focal area—they are quite a different shape from the bare branches of the trees.

Green Mansions by Elizabeth Barton, 60″ × 36″

In this quilt the focal area is indicated by a change in the way the lines go as well as in the values, even though the latter is quite subtle.

Line

If all the lines in a quilt are straight except one that is curved or spiked, that's the one that would stand out. The contrast of the expected with the unexpected is what draws your attention. This is evident in many aspects of life—think about the doctor looking at an EKG pattern. He is looking for an unexpected line quality. And in terms of shapes, the radiologist is looking for unexpected shapes. Of course, such focal areas as those are ones we would rather not have!

For some other examples: In *Kite* (page 36), the focal area is indicated by a change in direction of the main lines as well as a change in value and color. In *What Pretty Smoke* (page 50), attention is drawn to the distant chimney by the diagonal lines forming a tent shape over it.

Rainy, Rainy Night by Elizabeth Barton, 59″ × 35″

Value

The focal area should have the highest value contrast. Value is really the most important element when it comes to pulling attention—often from right across the room: the gleam of light in the dark forest, the lamplight along the edge of a profile (something that Rembrandt used a lot). You will always see the area where the lightest lights and the darkest darks come together. Be careful not to have areas of high value contrast in supporting roles, for example toward the outside edges of a quilt. It's especially important not to have a spot of bright white and black way off in a corner by itself; not only will viewers wonder what is going on over there, but they might ignore the important bit in the middle and feel confused. It's unbalancing in the art and for the viewer.

Note: For more on value, see Step 4: Value (pages 51–56).

Nantahala by Elizabeth Barton, 31″ × 47″

In both these quilts, the use of a high contrast between some of the lightest and the darkest values in the piece draws attention to the major focal area.

Color

As with shape, line, and value, if you want to draw attention to something, make it a different color. This works especially well if the color is also much more intense in the focal point than in the nonfocal area. Look at many paintings and you'll see how the artists will have just a few little spots of highly saturated, intense color, such as a bold orange or a bright fuchsia, right in the key area. That's not an accident. And it's not because the key person just happened to be wearing an orange hat. It's because the artist is saying, "Now look here! This bit is really important." A couple of spots of a really bright, bold color will always make us peer more closely at that point—one little clump of berries on a holly bush, the cherry on the ice cream sundae, and such. Actually the cherry draws our eye because its shape is different (much rounder and more defined, with crisper edges), because its color is deeper and richer than that of the ice cream, and also because its outline, with the perky little stem, is a huge contrast to the flowing lumpiness of the sundae. So for all those contrasting reasons it stands out.

Texture

A mistake I've often seen people make is to use a distinctly patterned, highly textured fabric in a section of the quilt that should be the background, such as the sky or the distant mountains. They'll think the fabric is perfect because maybe it has mountain forests printed on it, or a bold batik sky pattern. But what happens instead is that fabric, having the most distinct texture, will really draw the eye because of its contrast with more subtle fabrics. If a quilt is mainly solids or very small, gentle prints, use the clear and obvious print for something in the foreground, or for the focal area, but not in the background.

Meadow Farm by Elizabeth Barton, 46" × 23"

In *Meadow Farm*, the eye is drawn to the pale yellow area because it is different from the mainly green and pink tones used elsewhere in the piece.

Track of Vision

It's important to make sure that viewers look at all parts of a quilt. Obviously they're going to be most attracted to the focal area—you planned for that. But then you want them to examine the rest of the quilt as well. There are a number of ways of achieving this, and they have the added benefit of making the piece appear much more energetic. You want visual movement in the quilt, even if it's just the gentle to and fro of the palm fronds above the hammock.

Photo by Karen J. Hamrick

Photo by Karen J. Hamrick

What Pretty Smoke by Elizabeth Barton, 36″ × 43″

In this quilt, the eye is drawn around the piece by the bold yellow shapes that create a pathway up, over, and down.

Bluebeard's Castle by Elizabeth Barton, 18″ × 24″

In *Bluebeard's Castle*, I've directed the eye around the quilt by the use of line. You can use any of the elements (shape, line, value, color, or texture) to guide a viewer around a piece.

The way to do this is to use some device to attract viewers to move their gaze. We know that people are hardwired to see and be attracted by movement, so you want to create the illusion of movement in the quilt. Things like paths or roads that curve or recede into the distance look like movement; arrow shapes that point across the quilt also tend to guide us. Little shapes or lines of a very light value also set us moving along to follow them—"white lights lead to red lights," as flight attendants often tell us. Gradations also cause us to follow whatever is graduated, whether it's shapes that change, lines that get skinnier or fatter, values that get deeper, or colors that morph from blue to yellow.

One of the effective devices (probably not applicable to quilts) that classical painters use is the direction of gaze of the supporting characters. It's like a tennis match: You see all heads turning to look at something and you want to look that way too.

Wrap-Up

You can see that there are many ways of suggesting depth and of using the space within those first four lines (the edges) of the quilt. Don't be daunted by these, but think about them as tools to enable you to get your message across. You won't remember them all at once, so keep rereading and thinking … it's great exercise.

Step 4: Value

The Importance of Value

So far in this book you've just worked on some possible design sketches using only shape and line. These are the first two elements, or tools, you have to work with. Now I want to introduce *value*, sometimes referred to as *tone*, but since that word is less common and more vague, I suggest you stick to *value*, or *tonal value*. *Value* refers to the lightness or darkness of something. A dark value would be brown, black, or navy blue. A light value would be a very pale color such as white, lemon, or pale ice blue. It is important in a quilt to have a good mix of values; otherwise the piece tends to look bland. Unless your main idea is to make a piece about how bland life is, always make sure you have light, medium, *and* dark values.

DYEING FABRIC IN VALUE GRADATIONS

When I teach fabric dyeing, I always begin by having the students dye a range of values in the main color they've chosen for a quilt. Having such a beautiful range makes a great basis for a piece. It is often difficult to buy graduated colors in commercial fabric, but if you don't want to dye fabric yourself, you can usually buy hand-dyed fabric at quilt shows (and support the fabric dyers).

In dyeing graduated colors, you simply vary the total amount of dye powder or, preferably, dye concentrate (a prepared solution of dye powder and water, which is much safer to handle) to the amount of fabric. I use the Procion fiber-reactive dyes widely available from professional dye companies such as PRO Chemical & Dye (www.prochemical.com), Dharma Trading Co. (www.dharmatrading.com), and Jacquard Products (available in many art supply stores). For complete instructions on using the dyes, read through the directions on the dye companies' websites, which provide the best information.

The key factors are these:

- The temperatures at which the cloth and the dye solution come together—the solution should be in water that is 90°–110°F (think body temperature) to work best.

- The amount of soda ash you use to create the chemical reaction between the dye molecules and the fiber—I find 1 tablespoon of soda ash per yard/meter of fabric works well and is easy to remember. It brings the pH to 11, which is the desired level. Dyers add the soda ash to the mix at different times, but I find I get the best results if I wait an hour after adding the dye concentrate to the fabric.

1. Prepare a solution of 2 cups (16 fluid ounces or 500ml) of water to 5 tablespoons of dye and 3 tablespoons urea. The urea is only to help the dye powder dissolve. Of course different dye colors have different weights of powder, but for most art purposes (where exact colors are not so important) you don't need to worry about that.

2. Cut 8 pieces, ½ yard each, of prepared-for-dye (PFD) 100% cotton fabric, and place each piece, crumpled up, into a small plastic container or plastic bag (whichever is easier).

3. To the first piece, add just ⅛ teaspoon of dye solution in 8–12 ounces of 90°F–110°F water, enough to cover the fabric. To the next piece, add ¼ teaspoon dye concentrate in 8–12 ounces of water, and so on, gradually increasing the amount of dye: ⅛ teaspoon, ¼ teaspoon, ½ teaspoon, 1 teaspoon, 2 teaspoons, 1 tablespoon, 2 tablespoons, 4 tablespoons.

4. Wait at least an hour and then add ½ tablespoon of soda ash dissolved in hot water to each piece of fabric.

5. Wait another hour, or more, and then drain off the excess dye water, which should by now be exhausted. Rinse the fabric pieces in cold water until no more dye leaches out. I usually just steep the fabric in cold water overnight. Then wash in warm water in the washing machine using a little soap or detergent to prevent any back dyeing or bleeding. Hang until the fabric is damp dry, iron, and admire your gorgeous colors.

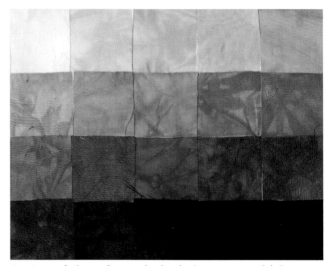

Create gradations of any color by dyeing your own fabric.

Check Your Fabric Values

Pull out all the fabrics in your stash that are the colors you're thinking of using. Divide the fabric into the different colors and then arrange each color by value. If you're not sure which is the darker of two pieces, one way to tell is to photocopy them in black and white. Or, if you squint really hard to reduce the light going into your eyes, you won't activate the eyes' color receptors. Another method is to look at the samples through a value finder or colored cellophane paper—red or green (because each is a medium value) usually works well. It isn't crucial to get the values exactly in order, so don't obsess about it. The key thing is to be able to sort them into lights, mediums, and darks, or into four values—light, medium-light, medium-dark, and dark—if you plan on shading your design sketches in four values (page 54).

Using Three Values

This exercise really helps you to see just how much a different value scheme can affect the look of a piece. Make six copies of the landscape or cityscape below (or both, if you're an overachiever).

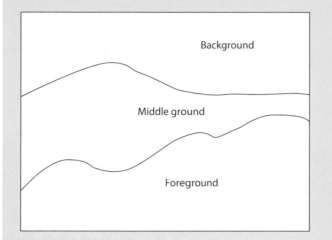

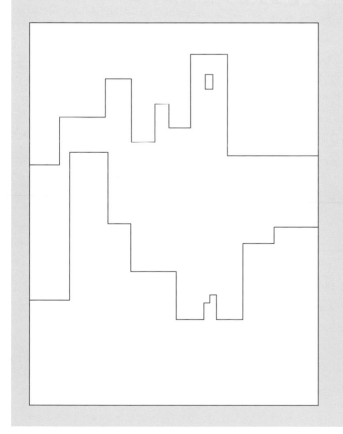

Use two colored pencils (or felt-tip pens) in the same neutral color, such as gray or brown. You want one to be of a medium value and one dark. Exact value doesn't matter as long as one is noticeably darker than the other.

1. Using the medium-value pencil or pen, do the following:

- Shade the background a medium value on two copies.

- Shade the middle ground a medium value on two copies.

- Shade the foreground a medium value on two copies.

2. Using the dark-value pencil or pen, do the following:

- Give one medium-value background copy a dark middle ground.

- Give one medium-value background copy a dark foreground.

- Give one medium-value middle ground copy a dark foreground.

- Give one medium-value middle ground copy a dark background.

- Give one medium-value foreground copy a dark middle ground.

- Give one medium-value foreground copy a dark background.

Continued on next page

EXERCISE **Using Three Values** *continued*

3. Lay out these six little landscapes or cityscapes. Isn't it remarkable how simply changing the values changes the mood and atmosphere? See if you can describe what those differences are. If you can classify them, then you can use this information next time you're deciding what values to put where in a quilt. I've often been asked whether a sky should be lighter or darker, or a certain section of a quilt lighter or darker. I think in order to find the right answers to these questions, you need to do a rough sketch and actually look at it both ways. *Make visual decisions visually*—don't try to imagine what something will look like, but look at the real thing instead.

4. Take another look at the six variations. Put them in order of how much you like the effect. Now try to figure out why! Consider whether the landscape or cityscape would have been as effective if the foreground, middle ground, and background were all medium value. If you're not sure, make another copy and shade it all in medium values. Your eyes will give you the answer.

5. If you have time, carry out this exercise in fabric too. Draw a little cityscape or landscape of your own and make six little variations. I'm sure they will be absolutely charming and will look great displayed together.

Of course you do not have to use just three values; experienced artists can differentiate up to ten different shades of gray between white and black. It takes practice, but anyone can learn.

0%	10%	20%	30%	40%	50%	60%	70%	80%	90%	100%

Value scale showing percentage of black

Tip You can also buy gray scale measuring cards from any art supplier.

EXERCISE **Using Four Values**

1. Choose one of the more interesting sketches you made following the instructions in Step 1: Inspirations and Design Sketches (page 6) and make several photocopies of it.

2. This time, use four values: light, medium-light (ML), medium-dark (MD), and dark. Again, if possible, use a neutral color such as gray, so you'll have light gray, medium gray, and dark gray. The unshaded sections will be white—the lightest value.

3. In the first copy, shade the values similarly to those of your original inspiration. If you find the colors in the original to be distracting, make a black-and-white copy to work from. It's often easier to spot the lightest areas first—try putting a little dot or a tiny "L" in those areas to indicate that they will remain white. Then squint at your original inspiration to find the darks. Once you've established the really light lights and the really dark darks, finding the two medium values, ML and MD, is easier.

4. On the second copy of the sketch, reverse the values: Light is now dark and vice versa, ML is now MD and vice versa.

5. On subsequent copies, try different things. Remember the effects you liked in Using Three Values (page 53) or just try random possibilities. Although this takes time, you can do it with your feet up watching the TV. Take your time and enjoy the process.

The Pattern of Light

When the sketch from either of the previous exercises is shaded, squint at it (hope I'm not causing you to squint permanently!) and look to see if the visual pattern created by lights and darks is interesting and cohesive. Do the lights form a kind of pathway? Are they in important areas—those to which you want attention drawn?

It's helpful to try to connect the lightest lights with each other, and the same with the darkest darks. Imagine the values as large puddles, pathways, or stepping-stones. The dark areas should lead to one another and all the light areas should connect, more or less. Don't worry about the medium values; they are the supporting chorus, important but not so eye-catching as the lead soprano.

You can lead the viewer to explore a piece by carefully manipulating the values (see Track of Vision, page 49). People tend to focus on the very bright or light values, and particularly on an area where the lightest and darkest values are adjacent (the focal point, page 45). This is evident in infancy: Babies like the high contrast of light and dark. This could be a basic survival skill because the baby will look at a person's eyes and eyebrows, the areas of highest contrast in a face. How rewarding it is when the baby's eyes focus on you! The caretaker or nurturer is thus reinforced to spend more time with the infant, ensuring the baby's survival. Well, our quilts are not quite at that level, but you can certainly gain a person's attention with careful use and placement of dark and light values.

Furthermore, it's good if the light and dark values are not dotted around like currants in a cake. A piece is more coherent if the values form a pathway or shape in themselves. In this way you keep the viewer looking at the whole quilt, both because there are interesting shapes everywhere and because they seem to lead one on.

Where Bong Trees Grow by Elizabeth Barton, 60″ × 60″

See how the light pathway (indicated in yellow) starts at the bottom left and then makes its way up to the top right, where it is brightest, around to the top left, and then back down.

As an artist, you want to engage viewers for as long as possible. Look at famous paintings in books or online. For online sites, try the Library of Congress, the Museum of Fine Arts Boston, the Fine Arts Museums of San Francisco, the Louvre, and the National Gallery of Art in Washington, DC. As you look at the masterworks in these collections, squint so as to see the dark and light value patterns. Notice how the artists have made the pathways and connected the shapes in fascinating ways. You will be doing the same thing in your quilts.

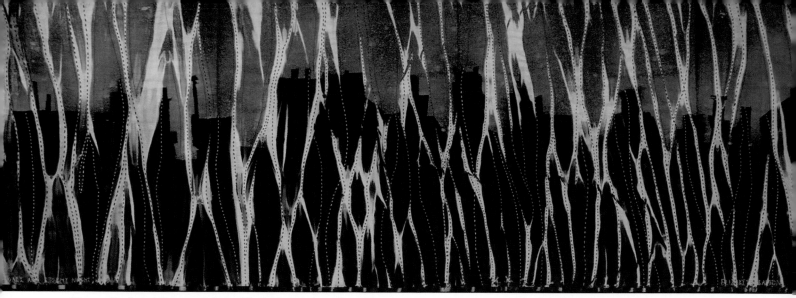

'Twas a Dark and Stormy Night by Elizabeth Barton, 60″ × 21″

Photo by Karen J. Hamrick

This quilt is low-key, using mainly dark values.

Please Handle with Care by Elizabeth Barton, 39″ × 48″

This quilt is an example of a high-key quilt using mainly light values.

One Predominant Value

A piece should have one predominant value to support unity. You can choose the dominant value to be light, medium, or dark. The choice really depends on the mood and the main idea you want to convey. What value do you think will work best for the piece you are planning? And which value will be the least used? An easy way to remember to vary the use of any element is to think of the Three Bears: Father Bear (he's big; there's a lot of him), Mother Bear (medium-sized), and Baby Bear (small but often with a great deal of impact).

Wrap-Up

Getting the values right is critical to both the sense and the sensibility of a quilt: The value pattern underlines the basic structure; the dominant value sets the mood.

Step 5: Color

Everybody loves color, but you must use it wisely to make the most of it. Like fire, color is a great servant but a poor master. It's important to know how to develop a great color scheme and to understand how color can work for you within a quilt.

The Four Variables of Color

Color varies in four ways: hue, value, intensity, and temperature. It's important to really think about these variables and plan for them carefully in a quilt.

HUE

Hue refers to the actual chroma or name of the color, such as blue, green, red, or yellow.

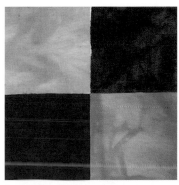

Four different hues: blue, green, red, and yellow

VALUE

Value is the lightness or darkness of the color. It's often easier to see values if you photocopy something in black and white. Notice the value when the four different hues are desaturated—the color is removed and only the value remains.

You can see that the yellow is the lightest, the blue the darkest. Red and green are both medium values, red a little darker.

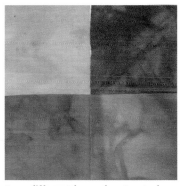

Four different hues desaturated: blue, green, red, and yellow

Some colors are usually lighter than others; for example, yellow is usually the lightest color. All colors, however, can vary considerably in value: You can have a light yellow and a dark yellow or a light blue and a dark blue. The dark yellow can be darker than a light blue.

Dark yellow and light blue, full chroma and desaturated. The dark yellow is darker than the light blue.

INTENSITY OR SATURATION

This term refers to the richness or pureness of the color. In dye terms, it would indicate the actual amount of dye powder used to dye the cloth. In paints, it would be the amount of pure pigment. Do not confuse saturation and value. Value is simply how light or dark a color is. Saturation or intensity is how rich and pure the color is. Very pale colors are not richly saturated with color, but neither are very dark colors, where gray or black has been added to deepen the shade. Generally speaking, the most intense colors will occur in the medium values.

Different intensities in three colors

Going from left to right as you look at the three colors to the right, at first the color is very pale; not much dye powder was used. In the middle you get the most intense colors: a lot of dye of one pure color. But then as gray or black is added to make the value darker, the color becomes less rich, less pure, and less intense, even though the value gets darker.

There are two different ways of reducing intensity when hand dyeing fabric. You can add a little drop of black dye, which has the effect of literally adding gray to the original color, or you can add a little of the complementary color, the one opposite on the color wheel. For example, if you add a little green to red, it shifts the red toward a neutral brown. It makes it darker, but the color is also less red, less intense. If you have some water-color paints, try experimenting with reducing intensity so you can see how this happens.

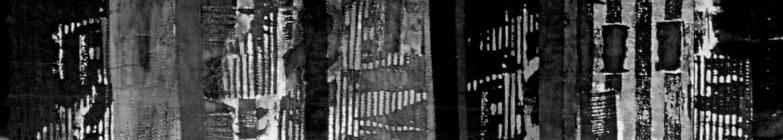

Color Intensity

1. Go back to your snippets. Cut more from different colors of fabric if needed.

2. Arrange them from most intense to least intense within color families—all the blues, all the reds, and so on. Look for the most intense examples of those colors, and then for each color find a watered-down or grayed-out version of the same color. As you pick up each snippet, ask yourself, "Is this color rich or dull?" Then as you place it in line next to other rich (intensely saturated) colors or dull (watery or grayed) colors, ask, "Is it more or less intense than this one?" It is helpful to look first for the really intense, knock-your-socks-off colors. Then look for snippets that are so gray that you can barely see a hint of color. You must ignore value! Remember the richest, most intense colors are usually of medium value and the least saturated colors are either very pale or very grayed and dark.

EXERCISE Color Intensity in Real Life

Go to your clothes closet, open the doors, and find examples of intensely colored and dully colored garments. Chances are the work clothes are duller (you don't really want to stand out) and the party clothes are much brighter. Queen Elizabeth II usually wears highly saturated colors in order to stand out so that people can see her. And most stars trooping into the theater on Oscar night walk the red carpet in bright colors. Intensity says, "Look at me! Look at me!"

When choosing fabrics for a quilt you have to be aware of the eye-catching impact of saturated color. You don't want it to dominate a piece; you want to use it wisely and sparingly, like salt or spice in a meal.

Don't worry if you can't do all of these exercises. The important thing is to improve your sense of color and your understanding of its properties so that you can use colors judiciously within your piece.

TEMPERATURE

Strictly speaking, temperature is not a technical way in which color varies, but for artistic reasons the temperature of the color is an important consideration, so I'm including a discussion of it here. The term *temperature* refers to the warmth of a color. Generally speaking, yellow, orange, and red are considered to be warmer than blue, purple, or green. This is because we associate red with fire (hot) and blue with the ocean (cool).

However, *within* a given color, you can have warm versions and cool versions. If you think of the colors arranged either around a color wheel or in a kind of extended rainbow, you'll see that there are various shades within a specific hue. Next to orange is an orangey red (warm red); then you have a scarlet, then a crimson, and then a fuchsia. Fuchsia is nearer to purple (cool) than it is to the orangey red, so we think of fuchsia as being a cooler red. Another way to think about it is to take a neutral red, like scarlet. Now add some orange to it—the red becomes a warmer red. Take another dab of scarlet and add a little warm blue like ultramarine. The red becomes cooler and moves toward crimson.

- A cool yellow leans toward green and a warm yellow leans toward orange.

- A cool red leans toward purple and a warm red toward orange.

- A cool green has more blue in it, whereas a warm green has less blue and more yellow.

- A cool blue has some green in it (it leans toward turquoise); warm blue (like a royal or ultramarine) has a little bit of red in it.

- Cobalt blue is considered a fairly neutral blue, but next to ultramarine (which has a little red in it), it looks cool. When next to turquoise (which has some green in it), it looks warm.

Cool   Warm

Fabric swatches in cool and warm versions of the same color

The Importance of Varying Hue, Value, Intensity, and Temperature

Do remember that while the various *hues* are fairly distinctive in their own right, the properties of *value*, *intensity*, and *temperature* (particularly the latter) are all relative terms. Why is it important to be aware of these properties? Because each of them can be manipulated to make your work look stronger, richer, and more eye-catching. Manipulating these color tools will bring life to the piece.

It's good to have a range of values, though you don't necessarily need a full range from white to black so long as some fabrics are lighter and others are darker. You can see the importance of value if you scan into your computer a picture of a quilt that is mainly made up of medium values. If you then increase the contrast of values (possible in most photo-manipulation software like Photoshop or Photoshop Elements), the quilt looks a lot more compelling. Look at the examples of the quilt *Foggy Day* (at right).

I've reduced the value contrast on this little quilt (*Foggy Day*) to show how the loss of contrast really makes the piece appear dull.

The Last Glow by Elizabeth Barton, 42″ × 42″

In *The Last Glow*, I introduced a tiny bit of a warm orange on the edges of the verticals to contrast with the cooler depths below. The warm bits make the cool sections cooler, and vice versa.

It's important to be aware of color temperature because, as the impressionist painter Paul Cézanne discovered, having a mix of warm and cool tones made the overall colors look richer. Cézanne spent many years trying to figure out how to combine colors to their best effect, and one of his conclusions was to place cool and warm tones next to each other.

The careful use of intensity is important because you want some intense colors to attract the eye, but if the whole thing is dripping in saturated color it will merely look garish. Take a look at Nancy Crow's quilts. She is a masterful colorist and nearly always

will include some neutral colors (those with very low color saturation) in her pieces. Including low-intensity or neutral colors makes the other colors look even more intense and rich.

There's a lot more about color to learn; I've just introduced you to the most basic outline. But I hope I've given you a clear sense of how color can vary and why you should know about it. I'm going to describe a few more technical things later in this chapter, but now is the time for you to have some fun and read about how to actually choose a good color scheme for a quilt.

Choosing a Color Scheme

There are two basic ways of deciding on a color scheme: using the color wheel / color theory or using an inspirational image. Try them both and see which you like best.

THE COLOR WHEEL

I think it's helpful to have a color wheel like the one shown below. This is a twelve-step wheel (the most common one), but there is also some research, by Albert Munsell, suggesting that in some circumstances a ten-step wheel might work better. There are no definitive rights and wrongs, however, so don't worry about it too much.

![Color wheel with labels: Green, Cool blue, Blue, Warm blue, Purple, Cool red, Red, Warm red, Orange, Warm yellow, Yellow, Cool yellow]

Color wheel

EXERCISE Make Your Own Color Wheel

It is a good idea to be able to draw a color wheel quickly for yourself.

1. Draw a circle—doesn't matter if it's wobbly; you can simply trace around a small plate or lid.

2. Divide up the circle up into 12 pie slices (more or less equal is fine). For the mathematically inclined, each slice of the pie would be 30°.

3. Label (or color) the slices: yellow, yellow-orange, orange, red-orange, red, red-violet, violet, blue-violet, blue, blue-green, green, yellow-green.

Tip Now that I have mentioned geometry and degrees, one little gadget I do suggest you buy (and I'm not keen on gadgets as a whole) is a protractor (because I love diagonals, I find a protractor useful for getting angles right).

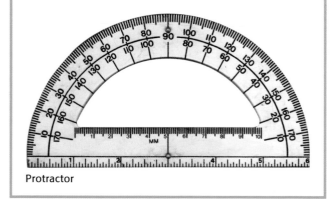

Protractor

In a Green Shade by Elizabeth Barton, 20″ × 28″

Color as part of the theme: This quilt is basically a portrait of my own house, which is in the woods.

Photo by Karen J. Hamrick

The Affluent Drainpipe by Elizabeth Barton, 37″ × 55″

Color as part of the theme: This quilt is based on the half-timbered medieval houses in England and also a comment on some of the black-and-white politics of rich versus poor.

CHOOSING A COLOR SCHEME USING COLOR THEORY

The first way of choosing a color scheme is to do it analytically using color theory as the guiding principle. Apart from monochromatic schemes, color schemes are classified mainly by their relationships on the color wheel. The most common and most useful color schemes are analogous, complementary, split-complementary, and triadic.

Monochromatic

A monochromatic color scheme is one (*mono*) color (*chroma*) used alone, but usually with varying values and intensities or saturation levels. The chosen color is sometimes paired with white for contrast, but it could also be put together with black. One color plus white is a traditional scheme for quilts. Red-and-white quilts were particularly popular, and there was recently a major show in New York City of a large collection of these quilts. My first quilts, traditional bed quilts, were all blue and white. One of my favorite monochromatic schemes, however, is black and white, and I've done several quilts like this. Sometimes I add just a tiny touch of a warm color. A monochromatic scheme is good for creating a distinctive graphic statement.

I've also made a number of quilts just using gray. I'm drawn to all the subtle nuances that can be achieved with a neutral color such as gray. There are basically two neutral colors: gray and brown. They are tertiary colors—a mix of different proportions of each of the three primary colors (red, yellow, and blue). Gray has a little more of the cool tones, brown a little more of the warm tones. Try mixing some paint and see what you get.

City of Mists by Elizabeth Barton, 40" × 52"

Milltown by Elizabeth Barton, 39" × 20"

Analogous

An analogous color scheme is three or four colors that are adjacent on the color wheel, for example, yellow, yellow-orange, orange, and red-orange or blue, blue-green, and green.

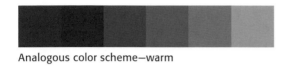

Analogous color scheme—warm

Analogous color scheme—cool

Analogous color schemes are good at conveying a specific mood. Just looking at the warm array above, don't you feel all cozy? And of course if you wanted to indicate the feel of a desert you'd use mainly warm colors. And if it's summer, doesn't the spread of cool colors look inviting? All cool colors convey different moods, depending on the subject, such as a cool day in the shade away from the heat or a freezing night on the open sea. And of course you can choose adjacent colors that have both warm and cool tones, such as purple, violet, and blue.

An analogous scheme is appropriate when mood is important. Interestingly, studies have shown that color choices evoke similar atmospheres and moods in most people.

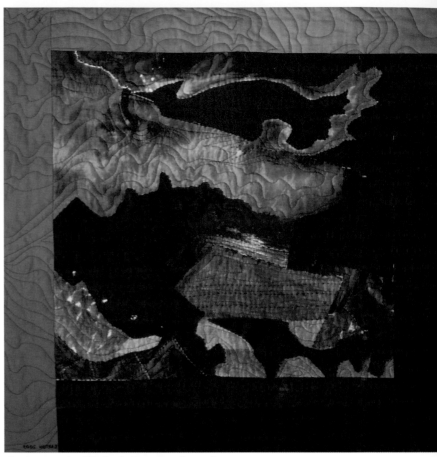

Fire Dreams by Elizabeth Barton, 31″ × 30″

Analogous scheme of warm colors: orange, orange-red, and red

Photo by Karen J. Hamrick

Green Houses by Elizabeth Barton, 47″ × 35″

Analogous scheme of cool colors: yellow-green, green, and blue-green

Complementary

A complementary color scheme is any two colors that are exactly opposite each other on the wheel:

Yellow and violet

Yellow-orange and blue-violet

Red and green

Red-violet and yellow-green

Orange and blue

Red-orange and blue-green

Complementary pairs

A *split-complementary* color scheme is simply any color plus the two colors adjacent to that color's complement. For example: yellow-orange plus violet and blue. Many paintings use a color scheme that is complementary, split-complementary, or some variation thereof. Start looking. You don't have to be too rigid about choosing the exact opposite color on the wheel or the exact adjacent colors. Some painters feel that the color that works best is often not the exact opposite one, anyway, but instead the one adjacent to it (as Munsell's color wheel would sometimes suggest). Many painters favor complementary and split-complementary schemes, for they are both rich and subtle, with contrasts of warm and cool hues and with bold interactions between colors.

I love the purple and yellow combination and have used it in many quilts.

Walmgate, November by Elizabeth Barton, 51″ × 64″

Meadow Farm by Elizabeth Barton, 46″ × 23″

Edge of Light by Elizabeth Barton, 41″ × 24″

Rusty Answer by Elizabeth Barton, 41″ × 24″

I've also deliberately challenged myself to use some of the other complementary schemes—see if you can identify them in the examples at the left.

Triadic

A triadic color scheme is based on drawing an equilateral triangle on the color wheel. Start with one color, skip the next three and use the fourth color, skip three and use the next color. Two examples are red, yellow, and blue or orange, violet, and green. These are bold and startling color schemes, strong and a little aggressive. They demand attention quite assertively. Triadic schemes are often used in print advertisements to catch your eye. A triadic scheme composed of primary colors alone gives a childlike simplicity but could also be brassy if intensely saturated colors are used. The triad of secondary colors— purple, orange, and green—is subtler but still strong.

Red, yellow, and blue triad

Purple, green, and orange triad

Triadic color schemes

EXERCISE Color Explorations

To do the following exercises, you will need small pieces of fabric in different colors so that you can make and keep the exercises. The exercises allow you to explore thoughtfully the ways in which color can be used so you can make your work stronger. I suggest you cut a 2″ strip from each of the solid-color (or almost solid) fabrics in your stash. You will use some of the strip for the exercises and the rest to start a fabric library. In this way, you will be able to see what you have—how many different hues, how many different values, how many different warm and cool colors, and the variety of colors and intensities. As you buy or make new fabrics, automatically cut a strip off to add to the library.

When you do the exercises, you can either make a sample for all the different color possibilities or choose as representative samples the colors you're most likely to use. The more samples you have, the better your understanding and appreciation of different color schemes will be. As you do the exercises, paste the fabrics on card stock, label each one, place them in sleeve protectors, and keep them in a file folder to create a permanent color reference. This process will not only reinforce your knowledge of the principles involved but also eliminate the chance that you will forget what that sample illustrated.

Color theory is not an exact science; consider it to be more of a guideline, and don't feel that you need to limit yourself exactly to these dictates. But color theory provides a good place to begin when you are choosing fabric for a quilt.

1. Cut squares from the strips of solid fabric and make examples of the following color schemes:

Monochromatic • Analogous • Complementary • Split-complementary • Triadic

Making a sample of all the possibilities will give you a greater understanding and appreciation of different color schemes you can have.

2. Paste the samples on card stock and put them into sheet protectors.

3. Label each sample to create a permanent color reference.

CHOOSING A COLOR SCHEME USING INSPIRATION

Working directly from a color inspiration picture can yield some exciting color schemes and is easy and fun to do. Repeat the exercise below with as many pictures as time allows. This was the method the amazing textile artist Diane Itter (look her up on the Internet and check out the Google images of her work) used to develop the color schemes for her pieces. And Alice Starmore (www.virtualyarns.com), the brilliant Fair Isle knitting pattern designer, uses a similar process.

EXERCISE Color Inspiration

1. Take one of the color inspiration photos/pictures that you have in your inspiration folder. Notice I say *color* inspiration, not *design* inspiration. *Note:* Collect some pictures just because of the fabulous range of colors in them: your own photographs, beautiful nature photos in a magazine, or printed versions of famous paintings.

2. From your color fabric samples, cut a square of every color that appears in the picture. Glue them down on a page adjacent to the picture.

3. Slide the page into a sheet protector and place in a notebook.

4. When you have time, make more examples. The next time you're making a quilt, you can leaf through the examples to find the colors that fit your theme.

Color scheme derived from a photo of the garden in full fall color

When working on color exercises, if you don't have some of the colors in fabric, color in a square with paint or a felt-tip pen, or use a paint chip from the paint store. Then make a list of colors to dye or buy. I dye all my own fabric and like to keep a good range in my stash. Whenever I see I'm missing something, I add the color to a list pinned to the studio wall. When the list has several items on it and I'm ready to dye, then I know exactly what colors to aim for in addition to just having fun sloshing color around. If you buy your fabric, take the list with you when you go fabric shopping and you'll find you will be more likely to buy fabrics you really need for your work instead of being seduced by all the fabulous new prints. Of course, you can allow a little seduction as well. . . .

The Importance of the Well-Chosen Color Scheme

Different color schemes are a little like different keys in music: Each one has a different mood or feel to it. That's why it is good to make an example of each one. When making a quilt, after you have settled on the main idea and made a basic sketch, you can think which color scheme will best fit. Be warned: Avoid literally following the colors in the original photograph; this hardly ever works and usually results in a dull or inharmonious piece. Plus, if you put a lot of effort into the dyeing (or buying), washing and ironing, cutting, sewing, quilting, and finishing, you owe it to yourself to put some time into choosing colors thoughtfully. Choosing a color scheme is where you put your art into the piece.

How Colors Can Influence One Another

When placing colors next to each other, it is important to consider how colors can influence one another. I will briefly review some of the main points, and then I suggest you make a few examples of them using the fabric strips you have already cut. If you're like me, you'll remember these effects much better if you've made some samples. Be sure to keep them in a folder for future reference.

SIMULTANEOUS CONTRAST

We manipulate simultaneous contrast all the time when choosing what colors to wear against our skin tone or our hair color, even though we might not be consciously aware of the process. When two different colors are adjacent to or overlap one another, the contrast intensifies the differences between them, whether those differences are in hue, value, intensity, or temperature.

Chromatic Contrast

Surrounding a color with its complement intensifies it. This means that if you want a color to look brighter and stronger, place its complement around it. For example, to make an orange berry look brighter, put some blue (its complementary color) shadows behind it. To make a yellow lantern stand out, put purple around it. If you want a red shape to be strong and noticeable, surround it with green. The two colors do not have to be the same value or intensity, by the way, and it often looks better if they are not.

Chromatic contrast

Temperature Contrast

If you want a warm color to look warmer, then surround it with cool colors. The contrast will make the attributes of each color more obvious.

Temperature contrast

Value Contrast

In the example below, note how the gray looks much darker against the white fabric than it does against the black. This is an example of a contrast of values making a color look darker or lighter.

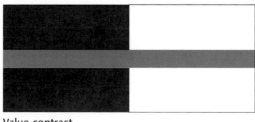

Value contrast

Intensity Contrast

Neutrals are so important. Using neutrals next to an intense color will really make the intense color sing.

Look at your color inspiration pictures or the work of brilliant fiber artists like Nancy Crow and observe the importance of using neutral colors (values of brown, gray, black, or white) to make a piece effective. The contrast evoked by surrounding an intense color with a neutral one makes the intense color seem brighter. For example, surrounding orange with gray, beige, white, black, or a grayed blue or green will increase the intensity of the orange and really make it pop. It will look much more obvious than if you surround it with an intense red, which is equal in temperature and saturation.

Intensity contrast

Neutrals not only make bright colors brighter, but they can also provide a place for the eye to rest. An art quilt is stronger if the colors are not all the same intensity. Contrast is vitally important, so be sure you have some neutral colors in your stash.

EXERCISE Simultaneous Contrast

It is helpful to learn the principles of simultaneous contrast by making some samples using snippets.

1. Take an orange snippet and glue it in the center of a piece of red fabric. Place and glue another snippet of the same orange in the center of a piece of blue fabric.

2. Look at the two examples of temperature contrast. Surrounding orange (a warm color) by blue (a cool color) makes the orange look even warmer. Surrounding orange by red (another warm color) does not alter the orange very much. Thus, if you want your orange bits to really sizzle, surround them with a cooler color.

3. Make samples of chromatic contrast, value contrast, and intensity contrast. Keep these all in a color folder.

Scarlet Town by Elizabeth Barton, 34" × 44"

For a warm, cozy feel, I used mainly red tones.

Choosing the Main Color for a Quilt

ONE PREDOMINANT COLOR

A good piece has just one main color. This does not mean you cannot have a lot of other colors, but one predominates, helping to unify the piece. You can choose any color you like, but specify to yourself exactly what it is. Choose the color by the mood and main idea of the piece. What color best expresses them?

Look back at the main idea you wrote down in The Main Idea or Theme (page 8) and decide what color should be dominant to show that main idea.

City of Willows by Elizabeth Barton, 47" × 32"

A city of willows sounded like a cool, breezy place, so I wanted to use mainly cool colors.

ONE PREDOMINANT TEMPERATURE

A good piece is predominantly either warm or cool— an equal mix of both is confusing to the viewer and unsatisfying. Decide whether the colors will be mainly cool or warm, make a note of it, and select fabrics accordingly.

ONE PREDOMINANT VALUE

The same holds true of value: Is this mainly going to be a high-key, light-value piece? Or is it mainly dark like film noir of the 1940s?

Dark City by Elizabeth Barton, 38″ × 54″

A low-key, dark-value piece.

Using Intense Colors

Use the more intense or saturated colors in the areas of the quilt that you wish to emphasize (see Focal Point or Focal Area, page 45): the most important or key points. Do not make the whole quilt from intense colors; they would fight with each other. Instead, have some intense colors, some neutrals, and some in-between colors. That way you will have some key players, some supporting cast, and some background scenery.

The Fabric

Now you know your palette—the dominant color, value, and temperature—so finally (!) it's time to pull out fabrics. Only those that are in your chosen color scheme, now. Don't cheat! You want a lot of different versions of the same color. If you have chosen yellow as the dominant color, take out every yellow you have.

Remember that color can vary by hue, value, intensity/saturation, and temperature. You want to include a lot of variation in these qualities of your chosen dominant color. Doing so will make your quilt much more interesting, so people will want to look at it longer.

When you have all the fabrics out on the table, divide them into four piles according to value: light, medium-light, medium-dark, and dark. This is when you will discover that you might be missing some values, in which case you will have to dye some or go down to the fabric shop. Oh, dear!

Wrap-Up

We all love color, but too many colors can have the same effect as too many rich desserts. Choose one color to be the star, and use it in different values, different temperatures, and different intensities. Allow other colors to be the supporting cast.

Step 6:
Evaluating Designs

How to Look at Your Sketches

The first chapter (Step 1: Inspirations and Design Sketches, page 6) describes several ways of generating designs. You looked at the design possibilities that could be derived from music, words, walks, and general observations. I asked you to be nonjudgmental, letting yourself explore your chosen subject matter freely.

Hopefully, you now have a design wall totally covered with sketches. I suggested while you were building up this store of sketches that you simply glance at them every day and move the less interesting ones down to a reject corner. But now it is important to *really look* at exactly what you have and make decisions based on what you *actually see*, not on what you *know*. In workshops, I ask students to talk about designs while the person who drew them says nothing. The reason for this exercise is that when you look at your own sketch, you see *not only* the sketch but *also* all the ideas about it that are in your head. When you are evaluating your own designs and quilts, you have to try to subtract the ideas and memories in your head and see only what is actually there on the paper or on the wall.

One way to do this is to try to see the sketch with fresh eyes, which can be done in several ways:

- Look at the sketch first thing in the morning.
- Stand with your back to the design and look at it through a mirror.
- Photograph it and look it on the computer screen.

Any of these ways of looking helps you to be a little bit more objective.

Another way to try to be objective is to look at the sketch purely in terms of its elements, describing the shapes and lines, *not* what those shapes and lines represent. A good design is one with a unified and balanced arrangement of shapes, lines, and values as well as a little variety for interest and excitement. A good design is *not* about how well the landscape, the building, the dog playing in the surf, or anything else is portrayed (no matter what anyone else says).

After you've generated these basic compositions, your next task is to assess the sketches a little more formally. And it's both a lot more fun and easier to be objective if you can do this with another person. Encouraging a friend or a group of friends to evaluate and critique with you gives all of you more opportunities to learn and practice these skills.

Don't rush this evaluation step. Sometimes I leave designs up on the wall for months because I've noticed that one of the best ways to judge the merit of a piece is to look at it over time. If it's still interesting and good to look at after months, it's a strong piece.

EVALUATING A DESIGN

The most important thing about a design is that the image conveys your *main idea*. Next, consider whether it is well pulled together and so engaging that people want to spend a long time looking at it. These qualities can be assessed by examining the structure (pages 33–39) and the adherence to the basic principles of good design (pages 77–84).

THE MAIN IDEA

First, assess each sketch in terms of how well it conveys the main idea. Asking others what they see is helpful because they can see only the sketch, not what is in your head. Ignoring that image in your mind is a skill that improves with practice. Your theme/subject/main idea may be a descriptive one, such as an image from a place you have visited. When you look back at your memories of Venice, Hawaii, or wherever it was, do you feel your sketch idea conveys your memories? Does your sketch embody that structure? When the piece is finished, would viewers be able to see not only the idea that inspired you but what you *thought and felt* about the idea? Can they see the mystery of Venice, if that was what inspired you? Or the reflections on the canals, if that was your main idea? Will viewers see the spikiness of plants in Hawaii in your design? Or the interlocking, thrusting shapes of the sky-scrapers of a major city?

The success of the design lies in how well it achieves its purpose. Remember that a design doesn't have to be representational or amazing. It could be about balance— how one big shape beautifully balances several little ones but with just enough of an edge (of tension or of mystery) to keep it interesting, like the sharp hint of citrus that accompanies the sweetness of an otherwise bland cake.

If you're not sure how to incorporate your main idea into a sketch, go back to the paragraph you wrote about it (page 13).

This sketch needs cropping to convey the main idea.

Are those specific impressions or some representation of them included?

Often a sketch needs cropping. While I liked the sketch of my mother looking in the wool shop at the top of the Shambles (a street in York, United Kingdom), I really wanted the quilt to be about the old street, not a specific shopping trip, so I needed to crop her out.

USING BASIC DESIGN PRINCIPLES

I suggest you critique each sketch that still looks promising after the "time" test (maturing over a few days on the design wall). Intuition, alas, can go only so far. Some people instinctively feel something is "right" or "wrong" but, in my experience, can rarely tell you why. If it's "wrong" and you do not know what's wrong, you can't fix it. Also, instinct and intuition are not magical talents with which a lucky few are born; they are actually skills developed over time. The more you exercise your critical faculties, the stronger they will be. Many people tell me they can't see whether a design or a completed quilt is "any good" or not. But with knowledge and experience you can gradually learn these things. So please don't feel that if you weren't born with intuition you're sunk! It is an acquired skill.

It's important to evaluate a quilt at every stage in the process. Use the basic principles of good, strong design as a checklist. These principles are usually summarized under the following headings:

- Unity and harmony

- Variety and tension

- Balance and proportion

- Repetition, rhythm, and movement

- Economy

Sometimes you'll see these principles described or labeled a little differently—the exact terms don't matter. All the books and the writings I've examined on this topic cover these same basic ideas, so I've used most of the terms you might come across in order to give you a complete vocabulary. You need words to think!

Unity and Harmony

This is the first and most important principle. Having an underlying structure (pages 33–39) is part of achieving unity, but there is more. Always assess every shape or line in terms of whether it's necessary to convey the main idea. Say you're making a quilt about the sunset behind winter trees (I can see sunsets only in winter, when the leaves are off the trees, and they are amazing, so this is a significant inspiration for me). But if you actually look literally at the scene out your window, you can also see a birdbath. The shape of the birdbath is strikingly different from that of a tree. Including the birdbath would be awkward—its shape is different, its meaning is different, its colors are different. Even though it's there in real life, to include it in a piece about trees would lead to a lack of harmony. The different shapes and lines in a sketch should look as if they really belong together. Think about art quilts you have seen that were not terribly successful because there were too many different things going on.

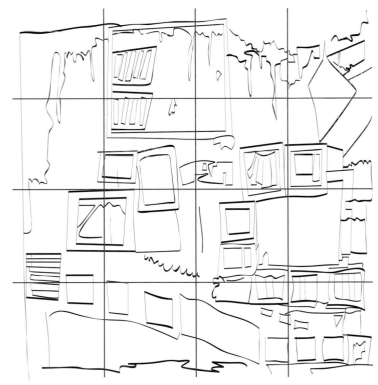

In this sketch, there is no unity; the shapes are quite disorganized.

Assess unity by checking each of the elements listed below. For each element choose a *limited* number of different examples of that particular element and repeat them. Choose according to your theme. For example, if your theme is buildings, then you would choose to work mainly with rectangles, using an occasional contrasting shape (like a dome) for variety. If the mood you're conveying is one of calmness, then your main color would be a calm color, such as soft blue or green, with just a little contrast here and there.

SHAPE

How many different shapes are you using? If all your shapes are different, the piece will not be easily unified. Look at *Windows: Blue Light* (at right), whose shapes all relate to each other.

LINE

Lines come in many different shapes and sizes: thin to fat, straight to curved to jagged. They indicate direction across the quilt: horizontal, vertical, diagonal, and circular. Unity is aided by some repetition of the types of lines you use. Frequently with quilts, these lines occur more with the machine quilting (see Quilting, page 106).

VALUE

Value refers to the lightness or darkness of the different shapes and lines in a quilt. While it's desirable to have a good contrast in values, in order to preserve unity, one value should be dominant; a quilt should be predominantly light, medium, or dark in value. Choose the value that best supports the theme.

COLOR

Choosing one main color helps to unify the piece. You can have plenty of subordinate colors for variety.

TEXTURE

Texture refers to the amount of visual texture. A solid-colored fabric has little texture; a soft, fuzzy print would be low in texture; and a defined, clear print has a high or dense amount of texture. In order to achieve unity, group textures according to some plan; don't scatter random bits of clearly printed fabric around the quilt. They will really stand out and weaken the overall harmony.

Windows: Blue Light by Elizabeth Barton, 40" x 53"

See all the repeated rhombuses!

Variety and Tension

If there is no variety or contrast in a design, then a quilt can be boring. Edrica Huws, the famous Welsh quilter, sums this up well: "It is splendid if there is some inner tension, a hint of disorder being controlled. That, to me, is the essence of an aesthetic experience." There are several videos on YouTube that you can watch to see her work:

> www.youtube.com > search: Edrica Huws Patchworks 2 and Edrica Huws Patchworks 3

Without some tension, a work of art is like a meal of white fish in a white sauce with white mashed potatoes and cauliflower. And white bread on the side. Think of a Nine-Patch quilt with every block containing the same motif, say, for example, the exact same leaf. Now, imagine that same quilt with the leaves in different colors, or having just slightly different shapes (like real leaves). It's so much more lively and interesting. Now just push those leaves around a little, so they're not right in the middle of the patch; perhaps some might even overlap a seam slightly. You could even have fun with one or two "missing" leaves that then appear somewhere else. Wouldn't that be a lot more interesting? Yet you've repeated the ideas of leaves within blocks, of the block shapes, and of the line edge quality of leaves, and thereby preserved the harmony and unity of the quilt. If there are no connections between the elements (whether shape, line, color, or texture), then viewers just get puzzled; if the elements are just a little different, even just one or two of them, then viewers will be intrigued and spend more time with the piece.

In this sketch for *Where Bong Trees Grow* (quilt is on page 55), the contrast of tree shapes with building shapes gives interest.

Think about a quilt in which every line is just perfect, so obsessively geometric that it is almost like a blueprint. Compare that with one whose lines and shapes are more natural, with a little curve here and there. Wouldn't the second one be more intriguing? These ideas apply to other art forms too. Rigidity versus naturalness is particularly evident in landscaping. I've seen plantings with the tulips in rigid rows, measured out the way a butler arranges the silverware before a state banquet! Such rigidity does not tell us anything about the nature of a tulip, though it might tell us something about the personality of the landscaper. Tulips are elegant and graceful, with sinuous stalks, and a quilt or painting about tulips should have elegant and graceful lines and shapes to convey that. If everything is exactly the same and all in the exact right place, the quilt lacks interest. The flowers don't look like flowers but are more like soldiers on parade. And even if you want to make a quilt about soldiers on parade, it would be much more interesting if one soldier had ears that stuck out or a twinkle in his eye.

Balance and Proportion

Human beings generally like things to be balanced; we feel safer that way. This is true even in the way we see art. Check to see if the large shapes in your sketch are balanced and spread out fairly evenly. Make sure there isn't a large mass that puts a heavy weight on one side of the piece, like a bigger boy on the seesaw with a toddler at the other end. If you find one, simply move it—even if in real life that dark, interesting shape was off to the side. Generally speaking, moving a heavy mass toward the middle will help. Remember, you are the artist and you can make any changes you want. Imagine the bigger boy moving toward the middle of the seesaw while the toddler balances right on the edge. At some point, they will reach equilibrium, and you can too. Landscape painters discovered early on that it often helped the design of a painting to move a tree slightly to the left or remove a bush completely. You can do this too!

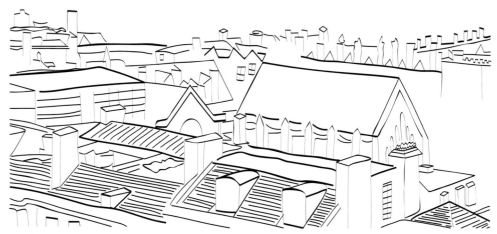

The large white shape is out of proportion to the other, more interesting shapes.

It is good to have a vertical balance as well as a horizontal balance. Unless your main idea is about the weight of the world hanging above us, it is better to have the larger, heavier shapes toward the bottom of the sketch. The main idea that you want to convey is the main determinant of how you arrange elements: The use of design principles should always support the theme.

Proportion refers to the relationship of the sizes of shapes. If you think about a Japanese garden, with stones, lanterns, and combed gravel, the sizes of the stones and the lantern should be in proportion. If the lantern is enormous and the rocks are tiny, they are out of proportion to each other. In a dollhouse, to achieve the right visual illusion of reality, it's best if the people, the furniture, and the appliances are at the same scale. While children don't care if the dollies have a giant iron that none of them could lift, it would look odd to us. A large lady looks better in garments with long, flowing lines rather than dinky little bows. I'm sure you can think of more examples.

Repetition, Rhythm, and Movement

Repetition aids both unity and variety. Use repetition to create rhythms and movement within a piece. A piece that has no movement is static. A piece with too much movement and no repetition is chaotic. The right amount depends on the theme, but whatever you have, that movement should be interesting, rhythmic, and controlled, supporting unity by pulling the piece together. Think about it in terms of music: Without a specific beat or rhythm, music can become chaotic and uncomfortable; with an interminable, solid, unmoving beat, it can be deadly boring. In making art you're trying to achieve a balance between those two undesirable poles: chaos and boredom. Chaos is fine if that is your main idea, but usually it is not.

Cropping and removing some of the extra shapes and rhythms often helps to reinforce an idea, as can be seen to the right and below.

The original photograph

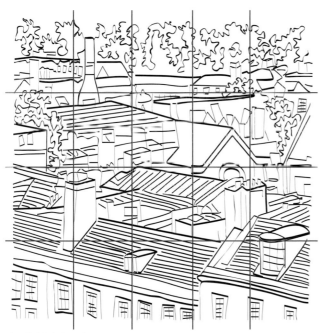

The initial sketch

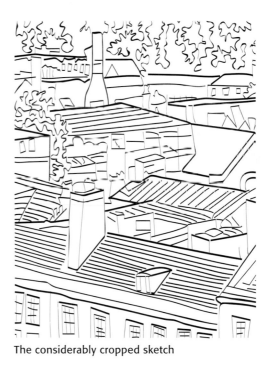

The considerably cropped sketch

City Blocks by Elizabeth Barton, 39″ × 41″

Repeating elements is a major strategy in achieving harmony. However, it is much more interesting if the repetitions are not too orderly. Think about a fence. Fence posts that repeat the strong vertical shape help with unity, but if they are too regimented, all the same height, width, value, and distance apart, the viewer's eyes will glaze over. Put a little syncopation into the spacing!

The different elements of design (shape, line, value, color, and texture) are simply building blocks. When working with sketches, you are mainly using shapes and lines. If your sketch has a lot of vertical or horizontal lines, or both (as in most architectural designs), the repetition of the lines provides unity. In a more natural scene, you might have repetition of curved lines. Repeating diagonal lines gives a lot of dynamic movement and activity to a piece.

Interestingly, we see each kind of line as having a different quality. Horizontal lines are thought of as being calm and serene. Vertical lines are strong and stable, or they could indicate growth. Diagonal lines are suggestive of forward movement. You can see how each kind of line, and what it means to us, relates to the position of the human body in space:

Horizontal: Serene; sleeping or resting

Vertical: Strong; standing, at attention

Diagonal: Moving forward; striving

In addition to lines, you can rhythmically repeat all the other elements. In *City Blocks*, I repeated many triangular shapes. Cézanne was known for repeating certain warm and cool color sequences in his impressionist watercolors.

Economy

Economy is one of the most important guidelines. A successful piece of visual art can be compared to a poem—every single word should add something to the meaning of the poem. While there will be connecting words, of course, there should be nothing extraneous, no filler added simply to take up space.

In this sketch, there's just too much of everything; plus, it's top-heavy.

It's important to check constantly, at the sketch stage and then again before you sew everything together, to make sure no irrelevancies have crept in. Many artists assess each component in a piece to make sure it's necessary. Either move it or hide it to see if it is necessary. Often the piece looks stronger as soon as you remove the unnecessary object. I sometimes teach a short workshop called Extreme Doggie Makeover. In nearly every case of a failed piece, removing something improves it dramatically. One lady was so keen to hang on to an element that absolutely didn't fit, that I had to wait until she went to the bathroom to remove and hide it!

Wrap-Up

The regular application of these few principles will help you considerably in pushing your work to the next level. I suggest you come up with a short series of questions you can pin up on your design wall and check at the end of each session of working on a piece (see the last section of this book). Remember that you can *ignore any of these principles, if you have a good reason for so doing; they are only guidelines. However, artists working over centuries have developed these principles, and their continued use shows that they help make the work of art memorable and long lasting.*

Step 7:
Putting It All Together

Determining the Actual Size and Shape of a Quilt

Now that you have the design determined, the values planned, the color scheme selected, and the fabric pulled out and ready to go, it's time to start work on actually making the quilt. The first task is to determine its exact size and shape.

SHAPE

You can change the shape of a design even if the sketch is already perfectly drawn. If, for example, you have a square sketch of trees and your theme paragraph stresses the height of the trees, then you might want to make the quilt in a tall rectangle shape. It's really easy if you have Photoshop, Photoshop Elements, or some other graphics software. All you do is scan in the image, go to "Image size," and change the measurement of the length or the width. If, for example, you are starting with a sketch that is 2″ × 2″, change the height from 2″ to 3″. If the software automatically changes the width to 3″ to match, simply uncheck the box that says "Maintain ratio" or "Constrain proportions." Be sure the quilt is the right shape before you go any further.

CHANGING THE RATIO BY HAND

If you don't have a scanner or graphics software, you can still change the ratio, though it takes a little more work. Imagine your sketch is 3″ × 3″ but you'd like to make it as a tall rectangle: 3″ × 4½″. Divide the size you want (4½″) by the size you have (3″) to determine the amount by which you need to enlarge the drawing (1.5).

1. Draw a 1″ × 1″ grid over the original sketch. You'll have 9 squares, each 1″ × 1″.

2. On a fresh piece of paper draw a grid of 9 rectangles, each 1″ wide × 1½″ tall.

3. Carefully copy all the lines of the first sketch onto the new grid, stretching them vertically to fit into their newly sized space. For example, if a line starts in the center top of the first square and goes to the middle of the right-hand side, just make the same marks on the new grid, but each time the line will be traveling vertically a little further.

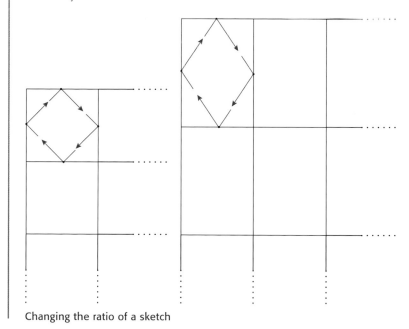

Changing the ratio of a sketch

SIZE

The most straightforward way to determine the size you might want the quilt to be is to measure the sketch, then multiply the measurement by 2, 3, 4, or more, and see which of the outcomes best fits your plan. For example, I usually work with a sketch 5″ × 8″. If I multiply the dimensions, I can choose which enlargement appeals to me.

To double, multiply both dimensions by 2: For example, a 5″ × 8″ sketch could be a 10″ × 16″ quilt.

To triple, multiply both dimensions by 3: For example, a 5″ × 8″ sketch could be a 15″ × 24″ quilt.

To quadruple, multiply both dimensions by 4: For example, a 5″ × 8″ sketch could be a 20″ × 32″ quilt.

And so on. Figure out which size quilt will work best for you, and then make a note of the number by which you multiplied the sketch measurements. This number becomes the scale on the sketch.

I recommend indicating the scale on your sketch in *bold* writing. It's easy to make errors if you don't constantly remind yourself, for example, "This shape is 2″ × 3″ [or whatever it is] on the sketch, and my scale is 1″ = 4″. Therefore I must multiply by 4. Let's see, 2 × 4 = 8 and 3 × 4 = 12. Therefore I must cut out that shape 8″ × 12″." I actually find it helpful to say this out loud to myself as I'm cutting. If you talk to yourself, you know you are talking to an intelligent person!

So write the scale—1″ sketch = 3″ quilt (or 4 or 5, whatever you chose)—large and clear on your sketch!

Continuous Evaluation

Building a quilt on the wall is exciting, but take your time and do it slowly and carefully. It is important to stop and look frequently. Ask these questions: Does that look right? Is the balance good? Is everything related? Is there anything that is out of place (even though it is a gorgeous bit of fabric)? Refer to the notes you made when you read through Using Basic Design Principles (pages 77–84). Look at the checklist I suggested on page 77, and add your own personal quality control items because *you* know *your own* strengths and weaknesses. Some people are overinclusive, others are too safe in their choices, and so on. While I've heard it said that planning like this takes the fun out of the process, for me it's not the fun I lose but rather the frustration I gain if I stray far from my original intention and make a total catastrophic mess on the wall.

Enlarging the Design Using a Grid

From this point, it's easier to work with a copy of the sketch that does *not* have the values shaded in. First, draw a grid over the sketch (I use 1″ × 1″, but use whatever makes the most sense to you). In the sketch below, I've drawn the grid in red so I don't confuse sketch lines with grid lines. When the piece is fairly small, like this one, I find it easier to draw the grid in half-inches rather than inches. You can, of course, choose whatever makes the most sense to you.

My sketch is 2½″ × 5″, and I want the quilt to be 10″ × 20″; therefore 1″ on the sketch equals 4″ on the quilt. As you can see, I've indicated the scale on the grid and also written the quilt measurements along two sides and the actual sketch measurements on the other two. This helps to keep me on track. With the grid in place I can calculate the size and placement of the fabric pieces I will cut for the quilt. I usually work from the actual quilt measurements that I've indicated on the sketch (on the left and bottom); that way I make fewer mistakes!

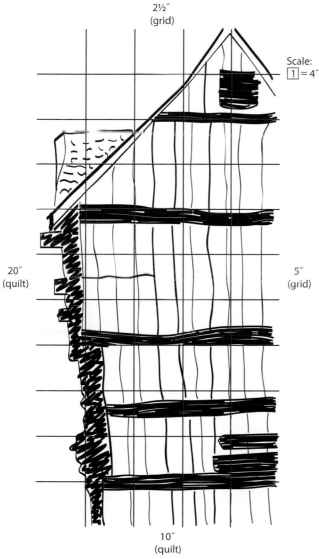

Gridded sketch

Blocking Out the Quilt in Fabric
THE BASE

Cut a piece of fabric to be the base upon which you will build the quilt. A single piece of fabric behind the whole quilt helps it to stay square and flat. If you're short of fabric, you can sew several pieces together. If you find the quilt top is too bulky in the end, you can trim away excess fabric from the back.

You can use any of the following for the base:

- A piece of very lightweight interfacing. The kind that has a grid printed on it makes positioning easy, but it isn't always available. Don't use the fusible kind, though, because when you start to iron, it will fuse to things you might not want; plus, you can't trim it away later. Use interfacing when your design doesn't have one single piece of background fabric behind all the others.

- A spare piece of any lightweight fabric you have.

- A piece of the fabric that will form the background to the quilt, even though much of it will be covered by the other pieces. For example, in a landscape quilt, this could be the sky fabric—it might appear just at the top and through the trees in the middle and then be a support behind the other fabrics in the lower half of the quilt.

- Pieces that you sew together to make a background. I have sewn a large piece of "sky" fabric to a piece of "ground" fabric to form the base upon which I'll build a quilt. In *Cement Works* (design wall series, page 90; finished quilt, page 94), I sewed three pieces together for the background.

Cut the base fabric about 1″ bigger on all sides than you need, to allow for error (I always have errors!).

Pin the base fabric up on the design wall.

Plumb Line

I like to hang plumb lines beside my base piece to keep everything straight. I really hate quilts with wobbly edges. To make a plumb line, attach a small weight (such as a metal bobbin) to a piece of cord, a ribbon, or a length of ripped-off selvage, and pin the other end to the design wall alongside the base.

> **Tip** Always rip off selvages—they are hard to sew through and stretch differently from the rest of the fabric.

Fabric

The fabric you pulled out earlier when you chose the color scheme should be sorted into four piles by value (assuming you have four values on your sketch— if you have more, or less, adjust the fabric piles accordingly).

This is *all* the fabric you will work with. No diving into the storage boxes under the table. Why? Because you have carefully chosen all the fabric for this piece bearing in mind all considerations. Nine times out of ten, if you suddenly pull out a different piece of fabric from your stash, it won't work. It wasn't part of the original plan. The value-shaded sketch is the plan, and it's helpful to have it on the wall next to where you will build the quilt. Keep the gridded copy of the sketch on the cutting table. You are ready to begin.

Fabric sorted into values

The same fabric as above, desaturated to make sure that the values are correctly sorted

---

Building the Quilt Layer by Layer
BACKGROUND

Note: If the base fabric is the background, you can begin placing the shapes on the background (page 90).

I suggest you construct the top mainly using appliqué techniques, unless a section is easily pieced. My foregrounds are usually appliquéd, but sometimes I want a pieced background, and I do that piecing before pinning anything else up on the wall.

It's easier to work from back to front and top to bottom. Begin with the rearmost background piece, cut it to size, and pin it onto the design wall on top of the base fabric. The background piece is the fabric that is behind everything else. In an outdoor representational piece this is usually the sky; in an interior scene it might be the wall of the room—unless there's a window with trees beyond, in which case, it's the trees. If the design is abstract, look for the color that appears behind everything else.

How do you know what size to cut? Look at your sketch.

1. Look for the highest point at which that particular fabric appears.

2. Look for the lowest point where you can see that same fabric in the gridded sketch.

3. Count up the inches the piece covers from the lowest point to the highest point. Multiply that by the scale.

4. Add on a little bit (½″ for a small piece, 1″ for a large piece) where you need extra to go under the pieces that will go on top. *Note*: You only need a little extra for an underlap for the first few pieces, where you are building up the background.

5. Count up the inches the piece covers from the leftmost point to the rightmost point. Again add on a little bit to allow for the fabric to go beneath the other fabrics, so that you have something to appliqué the other layers onto.

Tip Allowing extra for underlap is only necessary for shapes that are behind other shapes. As long as you don't have holes, you are all right. If you like to cut *each* piece larger to allow for a seam allowance, that's fine. However, *always* iron the seam allowance under before pinning the fabric shape onto the quilt. If you don't, you can't see the piece as it will be when it's all sewn together, and thus you can't evaluate the balance between one piece and another. I rarely bother with seam allowances unless I'm cutting a very long, straight piece of fabric that frays easily. Use your own personal taste and judgment on this one.

THE SHAPES ON TOP OF THE BACKGROUND

Repeat the measuring. It's fine to be approximate; a quilt is much more painterly if it's a little looser than the sketch. Cut out and pin every piece of fabric until you have everything cut out and positioned.

Following is a series of photographs of *Cement Works* being gradually built on the design wall. The quilt is based on a photo of an old cement factory in my hometown.

1. Blue background has been pieced. The first shape, one that lies behind the others, has been cut out and pinned.

2. Several more shapes have been added and relationships between them adjusted—partly as in the sketch and also as to how they looked when up on the wall.

3. Two more shapes have been added, but I'm not sure about the black on the left; I think it's too dark and too strong.

4. I've tried a light gray instead and put in the first connecting gantry.

5. The light gray was too weak for that position, so instead I've tried a warm yellow over the black, and that looks good.

6. I've added in more gantries and connected the main shapes. I've connected the ladder shape to the big elevators on the left and also to the base for the right-hand shape.

7. I didn't like the first gantry—it was too heavy; tried a lighter one, and another base on the right.

8. I still didn't like the gantry and decided to try using separate yellow triangles that the eye will connect.

As you can see, there are still a lot of decisions to be made when building the quilt on the wall, but the placement of the main large shapes and the main values were decided in the initial sketch, so I know the structure is sound.

9. I like the yellow triangles and therefore removed the black-and-white strip, which is distracting.

10. I've added more yellow triangles for the other gantry.

11. Details, shading, and small connections have been added in.

12. I've continued the second yellow-triangle gantry to the top, adding more details and more shadows to connect all the different shapes.

13. I've decided on a low background to connect those big shapes—they're still tending to float apart. In addition, I have added a little detail on the large yellow rectangle on the left to make it more interesting.

Cement Works by Elizabeth Barton, 42″ × 40″

Though I had a fairly detailed sketch, there was a lot of room for trial and error and quirky little interesting bits. However, the big decisions had already been made and the main structures in the composition carefully planned. I began with a pieced background and then gradually pinned the other shapes on top. When everything was adjusted as best I could, then I sewed it all together. Sometimes I tried a piece and really didn't like the way it looked, so then I had to backtrack a little. Creative discussion and decisions continued throughout the making of the quilt.

CHOOSING THE FABRIC FOR EACH SHAPE

Follow your value sketch to choose each piece of fabric. If a light value is indicated on the sketch, select fabric from the light pile. If the sketch indicates a medium-dark, then select from that pile, and so on. Actually, it is fun to do this with your eyes shut (yes, really). You can get some interesting results, and the design will work because if the values are right, the composition is right. Look at the work of Edrica Huws (see Variety and Tension, page 79), a painter who later in life made her pictures from fabric. She worked almost totally by value, and the images are strong and compelling, beautifully composed, and quite engaging.

SEAM ALLOWANCES

Most art quilters stitch their work together with raw-edge appliqué, a technique in which you don't need to worry about seam allowances. If, however, you want to turn under the raw edges, add your preferred seam allowance to each shape *before* you cut it. Iron the seam allowance under *before* you place the shape onto the design wall; otherwise, you will not see the composition on the wall *as it will be when it's finished*. All the relationships will change as pieces shrink. And it is vital to check the composition one more time before you sew everything together. Also, if you are going to turn under a seam allowance, it's easier to turn it under before you pin it on instead of having to take the piece apart to do it at the end.

THE BENEFITS OF BLOCKING OUT

Assembling the quilt piece by piece on the design wall is called *blocking out*. Since nothing is yet sewn together, nothing is fixed and anything can be changed. It's important to review the piece as you go along. You can change any elements of the composition that are not working. Rarely will you get everything right the first time. I never do! I usually look at the developing quilt critically at the beginning and end of every work session. When everything is pinned up, critique it thoroughly. I suggest you add to the considerations in Evaluating a Design (pages 75–84) any questions that relate to particular problems that you've had in the past. Don't sew the top together until you are completely happy with it.

Final Assessment before Sewing

When everything is together, it's time for a second major evaluation and critique. This time you are assessing how the piece as a whole looks when translated into fabric. Look at the quilt from near and far: a close distance, across the room, and even outside the room through a window (if you can). A piece should look good from every viewpoint. It's helpful to photograph it and look at it on the computer. On the screen, you can also look at the piece upside down and sideways. Looking at it in different orientations helps you to evaluate the piece simply as an arrangement of elements (shapes, lines, values, and so on) without the distraction of knowing what they are supposed to represent (if anything). Other ways to get some distance are to turn your back on the piece and look in a hand mirror, to look through binoculars the wrong way, or to use the wrong end of a door peephole or a reducing glass (often found at quilt stores for just this purpose).

If you're uncertain whether fabric A or fabric B is better in a specific place, take a photograph each way and then examine the photographs side by side on the computer. Seeing the two options like this makes it much easier to pick the better one. Remember, make visual decisions visually.

Don't rush the evaluation step. Let the piece hang on your design wall for a few days at least. Glance at it at regular intervals; sneak up on it and get a quick look. Ask yourself the Checklist and Troubleshooting questions (pages 96–101)—you may even want to write them out *in your own words* (that way it's more meaningful to you and your kind of work) to make a checklist for yourself to use at this stage in every quilt you make from now on.

CHECKLIST AND TROUBLESHOOTING

- Do the different elements (shapes, lines, and so on) go together?

- Do they all belong to the same piece?

- Is there one shape or one color that your eye keeps being drawn to? Is that something intentional, for example, in the focal area, or unintentional? If the latter, get out the ax!

- Are there areas that compete for attention? Sometimes you have two wonderful sections but they don't really go together: Pull one out and use it to start another quilt.

- Does the design have unity? Does it all look as if it is part of the same piece? (No bars of reggae music in the midst of a Chopin nocturne? If so—you know what to do!)

- Is there a preponderance of one color? One value? One shape? One kind of line? One type of texture? One direction? If not, decide which you want most of and be ruthless about removing the others. Make more units similar to the one(s) you like.

Red Shift 4 by Elizabeth Barton, 25" × 36"

Red Shift 4 is unified by the color and by the repetition of the square-within-a-square motif.

- Have you emphasized the focal area (if you chose to have one)? Are the contrast and placement appropriate? Remember the focal area is the most important and impactful part of the piece and relates to the main idea. If it needs more impact, use contrast (of color, shape, line, value, or texture).

- Do you have two areas of equal impact? One focal area is enough; two would compete and weaken the piece.

- Are there strong contrasts outside the focal area that are distracting? If so, reduce the contrasts.

- Does the quilt still engage your attention, or is it already becoming boring? If it seems boring, leave it under wraps for a few days; you may have been overly focused. Begin work on something else and come back in a week or two. Sometimes I leave a quilt top wrapped up for months!

- Are the shapes related, but with slight differences to catch the viewer's eye and add richness to the piece? If there are too many identical ones, add small shadows or highlights, or break off a corner here or there.

Castle Loch by Elizabeth Barton, 57″ × 38″

Castle Loch has a single focus—the castle shape itself.

Hostlers' Row by Elizabeth Barton, 40″ × 27″

In *Hostlers' Row*, a quilt based on a terrace of identical houses, I've tried to give each one an individual character.

- Would increasing the contrast (of *any* of the elements but particularly of value) improve the quilt top? Take a digital photo and use your computer to increase the contrast. Does it improve the piece? If so, don't panic, but consider adding a little bright spark of saturated color, to liven things up, and a few dark shadows.

- Are too many elements exactly the same and predictable? If so, just knock one of them a little sideways, change the color of one, flip one the other way around, or split a square into two unequal pieces and replace one part with a different fabric.

- Is this the piece viewers will remember at the end of the quilt show? If not, why not? Pretend you're a visitor to the quilt show seeing it for the first time. Memorable quilts tend to have something special about them.

- Can you see rhythms, pathways, arrows, or direction lines that move the viewer through the piece? If not, add a few stepping-stones of light (or dark), and leave an "entry" in the bottom of the design. It's generally said that a wall, fence, or solid line right across the bottom does not invite the viewer to explore much further. Now I don't know how true that is or whether it's been actually assessed scientifically. But if you feel like you can't get into the piece, then that's a possible solution to explore.

Overture by Elizabeth Barton, 35" × 47"

In this quilt, there are a lot of repeated lines and rhythms. You're encouraged to "step right in" with the steps up front.

Photo by Karen J. Hamrick

Strange Beauty by Elizabeth Barton, 55″ × 40″

In *Strange Beauty*, the weight of the steelworks is balanced with a lot of dramatic water.

■ Is the piece as a whole balanced? Is there equal visual weight from side to side? And is it heavier at the bottom?

Arrogance of Calm by Elizabeth Barton, 53″ × 29″

The colors, shapes, and lines in this quilt are restrained in order to balance the complex arashi (shibori) texture.

- Is there anything extra in the quilt that could be removed? If you're not sure, take a photograph of the piece with and without the piece of fabric you're unsure of. Compare the photos side by side. Everything that is in the quilt should express or support the main theme; extra stuff just adds … stuff.

- Have you asked passing folk (friends, family, the plumber, …) for feedback? Discussing a piece will often bring it into clearer focus for you. A work of art is a conversation between the artist and the viewer. But don't ask "Is it any good?" Instead ask open-ended questions: What is the first thing you see? Where does your eye go next? What do you think this piece is about?

Construction

Once you are sure the piece is right and looks good every time you creep up on it in the studio, then you can sew it together.

Note: While this book is primarily about design, I do want to share with you some construction techniques that are particularly appropriate for making art quilts of the type that I make. The following information is by no means complete, and if you need more specifics on constructing a quilt, there are many books and other references for you.

PLANNING AHEAD

Before you set to work on sewing anything, look at the quilt on the wall and work out a step-by-step assembly plan. Everyone has preferred assembly methods, and I encourage you to use the methods that work for you. The type of assembly technique is far less important than doing it neatly and having the quilt hang well when finished. This is a place to be practical.

Piecing

It's often possible to piece the whole background or whole sections of the quilt, regardless of how you are assembling the rest. Take a long hard look at the quilt and see if there are any areas that can be pieced separately and then pinned back onto the background. A cityscape, for example, might have several sections of windows that can easily be strip pieced. I like to get those assembled first and then pin those little units back onto the whole piece, since piecing is faster and easier than appliqué. But how you put the quilt together is really personal preference and depends on what works best for you. And if you should find you want to piece the background after you have already pinned several other elements over it (and yes, this has happened to me), I strongly recommend that you take a photograph of the pieces you have already arranged to use as a guide when repinning them on the pieced background. It is amazing how easy it is to forget where all the little pieces go. I know, I have done it.

Beehive by Elizabeth Barton, 39″ × 41″

In *Beehive*, there are several striped sections in the middle and foreground. I found it easier to strip piece those separately and then recut the shape: I cut long, narrow strips of each of the colors, sewed them together, pressed them well, and then redrew the shape of the entire striped piece before cutting it out again and pinning it back onto the design on the wall.

Taking the Quilt Top Off the Design Wall

After you have preassembled all possible small elements, pin everything together carefully so you will be able to lift the quilt top away from the wall and transfer it to a flat surface. My design wall is made from 1″-thick insulation board covered with batting, so the pieces are held onto it with pins placed straight into the insulation. When I am ready to move a piece off the wall, I run one hand up behind the work to support it while I retract each pin from the board and turn it sideways to pin fully into the fabric. As long as you have a pin on every piece, every corner and angle, and every few inches, pins work perfectly well. I never fuse any of the pieces. Pins can be used over and over again and furthermore don't inadvertently glue themselves to the bottom of the iron.

Having thus pinned the piece together and unpinned it from the wall, transfer it to a flat surface large enough to hold it so you can make sure everything is lying completely flat. There may be a few folds and bubbles that need a little adjustment. Then you are ready to carefully pick it up to sew.

Hand Appliqué

There may be some sections you want to appliqué by hand. You can do this before or after you sew the rest of the quilt top together, whichever makes more sense for you. I usually do this after I've machine sewn most of the piece because it's easier then to hand appliqué—and since I'll be handling the top quite a bit during hand appliqué, there will be fewer pins in it to fall out or stick into me, or both!

Gathering Storm by Elizabeth Barton, 44″ × 27″

In *Gathering Storm*, I wanted the blue silk overlay at the top to have an almost invisible edge, so I hand appliquéd that edge with one strand of embroidery floss in a matching color. On this quilt several of the little house shapes were pieced first and then appliquéd to the background.

Machine Appliqué

Raw-edge machine appliqué is now quite accepted even though in the past there was some prejudice against it by traditional sewers who were working from the idea that all quilts might end up in the washing machine and tumble dryer. Now it's just a matter of choice—you like it or you don't—so choose accordingly. Raw edge and turned edge are neither right nor wrong; it's simply what works with the piece as a whole.

There are a number of different ways to do raw-edge appliqué, so it's a good idea to make a few samples first. In one workshop, a student was unsure how she wanted to make the window units in her quilt. After discussing all the ways it could be done, she made a little sample of each method. Then she made a lovely little piece that was just the selection of sample windows. The study piece was charming, but also it served as a great guide for the future, whenever she might need to make a similar decision.

It's always good to look and see how others have sewn things together, so keep your eyes on this when you are at quilt shows. I use different methods depending upon the quilt, though I'll stick to one method within each quilt. I like a straight stitch with rayon thread in a matching color right on the edge of the fabric. I usually then go over this edge three or four times with the same thread when I machine quilt the piece. If I want to "lose" the edges I'll probably go with the straight stitch. But when I want a more definite edge I like a narrow, ⅛"-wide zigzag, fairly open, in a matching color of rayon thread. Very occasionally, I will use a contrasting-color thread with a wider, denser stitch if I want that particular seam to be a design element.

Art quilters Dominie Nash and Linda Levin also use a straight stitch, but theirs is about ½" from the raw edge of the piece. Try this on some spare fabric to see how it looks. They both use ordinary sewing thread. Carol Taylor does a wide, solid satin stitch around the edge of each piece in a matching rayon thread. Barbara Watler uses a fairly open, narrow zigzag stitch in a matching color. Jeanne Williamson uses a wide but not dense zigzag in invisible thread.

> **Tip** Because a dense stitch, such as that used by Carol Taylor, can draw up the fabric, it's a good idea to use a stabilizer behind the quilt top if you choose this method. Stabilizer is interfacing that does not stretch and will let the fabric retain its shape. The stabilizer can be torn or snipped away after stitching to decrease unnecessary bulk.

Some people fuse. I do not fuse because I do not care for the flat look that it yields, but there are a lot of people who do it well and beautifully. It is your choice. I must admit, I nearly always have a preference for a system that does not require me to buy extra stuff—especially stuff that can get stuck to every surface except the one it should be stuck to!

If you don't already have a favorite method, do make some samples and then decide which look you prefer.

Order of Assembly

Regardless of your selected style of appliqué, work from the back to the front, appliquéing all the pieces, whether single shapes or units, onto the background. When you are done, iron the quilt top well and leave it hanging on the wall for a few days. It is so easy to change or add things at this point that it is worthwhile making absolutely sure it is just right.

Squaring, Batting, Backing, and Basting

SQUARING

When all are sewn together, there may be up to four or five layers of fabric in places. If the quilt top is really bulky, I suggest carefully cutting away some of the excess from the back using a small pair of scissors, lifting the layers carefully from the back so as not to cut through to the front. And if you make a hole? Well, just appliqué on another shape! It will add to the uniqueness of the piece—no need to despair.

You can also trim away most of the excess fabric while retaining enough of the backing fabric to help hold everything square. As long as a substantial skeleton of it remains, excess fabric can be trimmed out, if you think it necessary. Trimming out is completely optional. I do it because I use a very old sewing machine that tends to balk if I am quilting heavily through a great many layers. So decide what will work best for you.

Before I make my quilt sandwich (quilt top, batting, and backing), I always give the piece a good press with a very hot iron. Then I make sure it is absolutely square, trimming off any extra. I use a 48″ metal T-square (also known as a drywall T-square) from the hardware store and a large square of acrylic or Plexiglas. You can get acrylic squares cut to size fairly inexpensively from a glass shop or a shop that specializes in plastics.

When I have trimmed the quilt top square, I sew a stay-stitch seam all the way around it about ³⁄₁₆″ from the edge.

> **Tip** You should decide whether or not to use a border when you *first* design the piece—a border is part of the composition. Most art quilts look better without a border.

BACKING FABRIC

Cut a piece of fabric for the back of the quilt, about 1″ bigger than the top. Press this piece well. Tape the backing right side down onto a table with masking tape at all four corners and the middle of each side, so it is smooth, unrumpled, and fixed in place. I use a solid-color piece of hand-dyed muslin, which is fairly easy to needle.

I set aside fabric from the same piece for binding/facing and sleeves. For the sleeves, I cut two long pieces of fabric for the top and bottom of the quilt. The top sleeve needs to be at least 10″ wide and the bottom 5″ or 6″. They should be the same length as the width of the quilt from raw edge to raw edge. Most shows require a 4″ easement on the top sleeve for the hanging pole, but I think it is wise to allow a little more. I have had sleeves ripped off and holes poked in them. I always attach a bottom sleeve, into which I'll insert a flat aluminum bar because I like my quilts to hang flat, straight, and level.

BATTING

Onto the taped-down backing fabric, gently layer a piece of batting about the same size as the backing. Batting can be polyester, cotton, wool, or any combination thereof. Each fiber has pros and cons, so choose what works best for you. I like my quilts to be really light to save on shipping costs, but also to have some loft so I can get some texture with the quilting. Currently, I use wool batting. If you are not sure what to use, send away to the batting companies for sample packs of all the battings they produce and make some samples to see what you like best. For art quilts, a thin batt is generally preferred. I do better with cotton or wool. I have discovered I am good at melting polyester. If you don't have a piece of batting big enough, it's easy to sew two pieces together, butting the edges, with a flat lacing stitch (like surgeons used to use before they discovered staples!).

BASTING LAYERS TOGETHER

Place the beautifully ironed and squared quilt top on top of the batting, centering it so the extra batting and backing extend an even amount on all sides.

Baste the layers together. There are a number of different ways of basting, but the simplest is straight pins. It's amazing how few fall out. The little safety pins have to be bought separately and then are hard to fasten with arthritic fingers. Also they seem to get blunt easily and can then tear a hole in the fabric. I have friends who swear by various glue sprays, but you have to buy those each time; plus I do not want gluey spray in my lungs. You can also baste the layers together with large tacking stitches. The disadvantage there is that you can catch those stitches in the machine foot when you quilt. So again, choose the method that works best for you. I do not recommend those plastic fasteners similar to the ones used to attach price tags to clothes; they leave big holes in fabric. My recommendation would be to start with the straight pins, and if you find you lose them, then try the little safety pins. Make sure they are small and sharp and do not put big holes in the fabric.

Quilting

There are many different ways to quilt, different kinds of threads, and a huge variety of texture possibilities, so choose wisely and bear in mind the theme of the quilt.

HAND QUILTING

If you plan to hand quilt or add hand stitching and there are a lot of layers in the quilt top, I suggest that you cut away as much as you can of the excess fabric under the top layer of fabric. I plan ahead with tops I want to hand quilt or hand stitch and make them from a cotton fabric with a regular thread count (80 or so threads to the inch).

Photo by Karen J. Hamrick

Hand quilting

MACHINE QUILTING

When I make a quilt from a high-thread-count cotton (such as Testfabrics' style 419, which is a beautiful mercerized cotton, excellent for hand dyeing and screen printing but almost impossible for normal fingers to needle), I always machine quilt, inserting a new needle at least once per quilt.

Feed Dogs Up, Even-Feed Foot

"Straight-line" quilting is done with the feed dogs up. The advantage of this method is that the stitch is even and regular, and you can vary your pace. However, you are limited to straight, or slightly curving, lines, and you can only go in one direction.

Feed Dogs Down, Darning Foot

Free-motion quilting is done with the feed dogs down (or covered) so that movements are absolutely free. You can go anywhere you want because the feed dogs are not continually pushing you forward. You can go around in circles, doodle, write, draw flowers or butterflies or long, slightly kinky lines—anything you want, and in any direction you want. The disadvantage is that since the feed dogs are not moving the fabric, you have to move it yourself and it takes some practice to do that evenly.

I do not feel that all quilting stitches need to be exactly the same length. I like the mark of the maker's hand, but there are a lot of traditional quilt judges out there who want every stitch the same. It is up to you to decide your own preference. If you want to free-motion quilt evenly, you need to practice a lot. And with practice, it's possible to sew quite a regular stitch. It helps to quilt to music with a strong, even rhythm; Bach or Mozart works well!

There are only a few secrets to machine quilting. The first and most important is practice! Many expert machine quilters advocate practicing a few minutes on a sample before moving on to the new piece to be quilted. Don't be afraid of it. Turn the speed of the sewing machine down to slow if you can, and move gently and rhythmically … you can do it!

Photo by Karen J. Hamrick

Free-motion quilting

Tip When you are quilting, make sure your shoulders do not rise up above your ears—keep them down so your hands and arms can loosely and freely move the fabric under the needle (and you won't get sore shoulders). And don't stay crouched over the machine for too long—take breaks!

MACHINE-QUILTING THREAD

I love the moment when I'm all ready to quilt and I get to choose the threads. I usually pull out about a dozen different ones. Consider your original main idea. I made a piece about water and the light on the water. When it came to quilting I wanted to bring out the light dancing on the water, so I used a metallic thread in a wave pattern. I used a different, broader and bolder, thread (Sulky Sliver metallic thread) that catches the light well to indicate the glints of light seen on the edges of the buildings with just a straight outline stitch. Then for the metal sides of the buildings I wanted to create a metal texture so I changed threads again *and* switched the needle to zigzag mode to emulate that strange pimply texture you see on metal.

For quilting I like rayon threads, which have a soft sheen and are attractive. I usually match the color of thread closely to the area I am quilting, unless for some reason I want to make a contrast. Thus, I change thread color a lot.

When doing free-motion quilting I usually start in the middle and work outward in every direction. If the quilt is large, I just roll it up. It's nice to have a wide table area all the way around the machine to take the weight of the quilt, but you *can* cope without. I only have a small table, and while it might take me a little longer and involve a little more shuffling around, I find I can quilt as large a quilt as I want. The important thing is to have the table at the right height so that arms, shoulders, back, and neck are not stressed.

Heavy Metal by Elizabeth Barton, 41″ × 42″

While a straight stitch is the most usual one for free-motion quilting, you could use something else. On this quilt I used a zigzag stitch to convey the industrial surface texture of beams and girders.

Detail of *Heavy Metal*

Bobbin Thread

I use a very fine thread in the bobbin and fill up about a dozen bobbins ahead of time. I prefer the color to closely match the backing fabric, unless there's a chance it could show through on top. For example, if the backing is dark green but the section I'm quilting is a very pale green, I'd switch to a light-colored bobbin thread. The top is more important than the back.

NEEDLES

Many machine-quilting aficionados recommend top-stitch, embroidery, or quilting needles, which have a bigger eye and a long, smooth scarf (the place where the thread comes through near the eye) so that the thread does not break so easily. Unfortunately, these needles are more expensive than others, so I usually test my stitching on a sample with a basic (universal) needle first. If all is well and the thread does not keep breaking, then I continue with the cheaper needle. However, if I do have problems with breakage, then I switch to a top-stitch or embroidery needle. Of course, you should *always* put a new needle in the machine for every new project. Machine quilting builds up a lot of lint since the needle is going in and out of the fabric frequently, so be sure to keep the bobbin area clean and lint-free.

MACHINE QUILTING PATTERN

It's important to consider carefully how you will quilt the top. Think about the quality and color of the lines that you will draw on the piece with the needle. I like to take a photo of the quilt, make copies, and then sketch out several ideas before I start. It's also helpful if you have some muscle memory from sketching the movements you'll be making, so practice ahead of time, first with a pencil on paper and then with the machine stitching onto fabric. This is also a good time to see if any adjustments need to be made to needle, thread, or tension.

Because free-motion machine quilting is a bit like drawing, you'll find it's helpful to look at books of drawings to see how various artists have used line to emphasize a design. You can make edges stronger by emphasizing them, especially if you use a contrasting color, or you can soften them with several passes of a blending color. You can use the stitching to add some texture or shading to a shape.

Formal patterns, like flowers or feathers, imported from books of traditional quilting designs are usually enormously distracting and out of place in art quilts. The quilting design is an important part of the piece and should be *unified* with it. Enhance the original idea with the stitching.

I like to begin to quilt in the middle. If it's a large quilt I'll roll up the sides so they fit into the machine and are not flopping all over. From the middle I work outward. I change the color of the thread frequently and use matching or contrasting thread, as relates to my main idea. Where do I want to soften edges? Where do I wish to exaggerate them? It's good to keep the amount of quilting fairly evenly dispersed across the quilt so you don't get any distortion or bulges. If bulges do occur, however, stitching over and over them usually calms them into submission!

Stop frequently and see if the effect is what you want. If it looks wrong, it's so much easier to have only a little bit to take out. If you have to take stitches out, do it carefully. You'll find obvious needle holes, but if you lay the quilt on a flat surface and spray the area gently with clean water and leave to dry, the squashed threads will plump up. Wait until the fabric is dry before you start again.

Ironing, Measuring, and Squaring-Up

Once the quilting is all done, iron well on both sides, working from the middle out to the edges. Then check again that the quilt is perfectly square on the edges. Make sure the width is the same at the top, bottom, and middle of the piece. Then check that the length is the same on the right and left sides, and down the center. If the widths or lengths are different, square up the quilt using the large T-square or square piece of acrylic or Plexiglas as a guide. You can also place the quilt on a large cutting board that has a grid printed on it, or even on the floor if the tiles are laid out in a grid. I squared mine on a vinyl floor printed with a 6″ tile pattern for years, until my knees gave out.

Once the quilt is absolutely square with all the corners 90°, the top and bottom are the same length, and the sides are the same length, it's helpful to staystitch the edges again (stitching ³⁄₁₆″ from the edge all the way around); this keeps everything stable and square, and will help the quilt hang beautifully on the wall.

Finishing the Edges

There are so many different ways of finishing a quilt with binding or interfacing that I recommend you use the one *you* like the best. If you like it and have used it many times, the chances of it being neat and flat are good. Binding should be unobtrusive, neat, and in keeping with the look of the quilt.

Epilogue

I hope you have enjoyed reading this book and that your seven-step journey to a stunning quilt is a smooth one!

About the Author

Elizabeth lives in Athens, Georgia. While a lake and mountains outside her windows would be wonderful, instead she enjoys many beautiful trees, which give endless seasonal variety. She grew up in York, England. There, she walked to school (one founded in the seventeenth century) along city walls built by the Romans around AD 71. Seeing every day the effects of time on buildings and landscape influenced her first quilts. Growing up in a dark northern city made light and windows extremely important. Many of her quilts are about light and the contrast between dark and light.

Elizabeth originally trained as a clinical psychologist and pursued this occupation for many years both in England and in the United States. Gradually, however, the idea of creating art from fabric grew ever more fascinating, and one year she just decided to let the license lapse and pursue art instead. While Athens, Georgia, has neither lakes nor mountains, it is an active art and music community, offering a lot of encouragement and support from the surface design professors at the university as well as opportunities for solo shows (of which she has had several). She began teaching at Arrowmont School for Arts and Crafts (Gatlinburg, Tennessee), then wrote lessons for online courses, and finally was persuaded to put everything into a book. And here it is!

Please visit her at www.elizabethbarton.com and www.elizabethbarton.blogspot.com.

Great Titles and Products

from C&T PUBLISHING and stashBOOKS.

Available at your local retailer or **www.ctpub.com** *or* **800-284-1114**

For a list of other fine books from C&T Publishing, visit our website to view our catalog online.

C&T PUBLISHING, INC.
P.O. Box 1456
Lafayette, CA 94549
800-284-1114

Email: ctinfo@ctpub.com
Website: www.ctpub.com

C&T Publishing's professional photography services are now available to the public. Visit us at www.ctmediaservices.com.

Tips and Techniques can be found at www.ctpub.com > Consumer Resources > Quiltmaking Basics: Tips & Techniques for Quiltmaking & More

For quilting supplies:

COTTON PATCH
1025 Brown Ave.
Lafayette, CA 94549
Store: 925-284-1177
Mail order: 925-283-7883

Email: CottonPa@aol.com
Website: www.quiltusa.com

Note: Fabrics shown may not be currently available, as fabric manufacturers keep most fabrics in print for only a short time.